It's easy to becom
allow its true mess
commercialisation, ~~~~ ~~~ in
Come and Behold Him, David Randall offers a highly
readable antidote to all these tired caricatures of Christmas.
Through the eyes of fourteen biblical characters, David
focuses us powerfully and precisely on the real Character
at the heart of Christmas, Jesus Christ. Whether you're a
Christian who struggles to get excited about Christmas, or
a seeker wondering what all the fuss is *really* about, this is a
beautifully written invitation to come and behold the One at
the heart of Christmas, Immanuel, God with Us.

ANDY BANNISTER

Director of Solas (Centre for Public Christianity), Dundee, Scotland

No part of Scripture is better known than the Christmas
story – and none is more widely misunderstood. Many see
it through commercial, sentimental, nostalgic or emotional
eyes, while secularists dismiss it as religious nonsense. David
Randall plunges past all of these and reveals the story's
dynamic, life-changing truth as seen through the eyes of its
prophets and participants.

Easy to read, enhanced by excellent illustrations and
thoroughly grounded in God's Word, *Come and Behold Him*
will open your eyes, stimulate your mind and warm your
heart. I strongly recommend it.

JOHN BLANCHARD

Preacher, teacher, apologist and author of 30 books, including
Does God believe in Atheists?

Does Christmas feel consumer-driven, or overly-sentimental, or even over-familiar? I heartily recommend this book as a refreshing and inspiring antidote! We see the story through the eyes of many different witnesses across scripture, providing us with a fresh perspective which is Christ-centred, faith-building and heart-warming – the best Christmas book I have read for many years!

JONATHAN LAMB

Minister-at-large for Keswick Ministries and IFES Vice President.

Can anything new possibly be said about Christmas? This little book answers the question with a resounding 'Yes!' Fresh and accessible in style, imaginative in structure, and thoughtful in its use of scripture and supporting illustrations, it will intrigue newcomers to the Christian faith as well as offering an antidote to jaded souls who think they've heard it all before. Highly recommended.

ALISTAIR DONALD

Chaplain, Heriot-Watt University, Edinburgh

One of the things I like to do during Advent is to ponder the all-familiar story of Christmas from different angles. I find there are always new depths to discover in exploring the mystery of God becoming human and living as one of us. So, I am delighted David has written this book. It will give me another great resource to help me celebrate Advent and Christmas thoughtfully and joyfully – filled with wonder and praise for Jesus Christ born in Bethlehem.

ELAINE DUNCAN

Chief Executive, Scottish Bible Society

Come & Behold Him

CHRISTMAS THROUGH DIFFERENT EYES

DAVID J. RANDALL

CHRISTIAN
FOCUS

Copyright © David J. Randall 2019

paperback ISBN 978-1-5271-0336-8
epub ISBN 978-1-5271-0398-6
mobi ISBN 978-1-5271-0399-3

10 9 8 7 6 5 4 3 2 1

First published in 2019
by
Christian Focus Publications Ltd,
Geanies House, Fearn, Ross-shire,
IV20 1TW, Great Britain.

www.christianfocus.com

Cover by Pete Barnsley (CreativeHoot.com)

Printed and bound
by Bell & Bain, Glasgow

Contents

Introduction.. 7

1. 'In the Little Town of Bethlehem'................................11
Christmas through the eyes of Micah

2. 'To us a Child is Born'.. 19
Christmas through the eyes of Isaiah

3. 'A Redeemer Who Lives'..25
Christmas through the eyes of Job

4. 'He Will Suddenly Come'..31
Christmas through the eyes of Malachi

5. 'I am the Servant of the Lord'......................................39
Christmas through the eyes of Mary

6. 'You Shall Call His Name Jesus'....................................45
Christmas through the eyes of Joseph

7. 'Good News of Great Joy'...51
Christmas through the eyes of the Shepherds

8. 'Where is the Child Born to be King?'.........................59
Christmas through the eyes of the Wise Men

9. 'Search Diligently for the Child'..................................65
Christmas through the eyes of Herod

10. 'Speaking About the Child'...73
Christmas through the eyes of Anna

11. 'My Eyes have Seen your Salvation'..79
Christmas through the eyes of Simeon

12. 'When the Time Was Right' 85
Christmas through the eyes of Paul

13. 'God Has Spoken'...91
Christmas through the eyes of Hebrews

14. 'The Word Became Flesh' 97
Christmas through the eyes of John

Come and Behold Him 103
Questions for Further Thought/Discussion

Appendix: Advent Readings 107

Introduction

'What can you possibly say about Christmas that hasn't been said many times before?' That question sometimes suggested itself to me in the course of nearly forty years of ministry in one congregation.

The basic story is familiar:

> *Once in royal David's city stood a lowly cattle-shed*
> *Where a mother laid her Baby in a manger for His bed.*
> *Mary was that mother mild, Jesus Christ her little Child.[1]*

But many extra things have been added to the story. Jesus *was* born at Bethlehem, but were there '*three* kings of orient'? And what about Christmas trees, tinsel and mince pies?

---

1   Hymn by Mrs C. F. Alexander (1818-95), intended to help her godchildren understand the phrase in the Apostles' Creed, 'I believe in Jesus Christ, conceived by the Holy Ghost, born of the virgin Mary.'

This book will concentrate on the basic message of Christmas, looking at it through the eyes of the various characters who (a) prophesied it, (b) witnessed it or (c) reflected on it.

Two things should be said at the outset. One is that, although we look through the eyes of various characters, our real focus will be – and must be – on *the* Character of Christmas – Jesus Himself. He is the central Character – the One who was born then, who lived and loved, who died for the sins of the world, who rose again from the dead and who will return to this world one day. 'In everything may he be pre-eminent' (Col. 1:18).

The other preliminary thing is that there isn't really any danger of running out of things to say about Christmas. Its message is inexhaustible. In one sense the gospel is simple: 'Believe in the Lord Jesus, and you will be saved' (Acts 16:31). Yet the apostle Paul who gave that answer to the question of what was needed for salvation would also pray that his readers might know the love of Christ – even though it 'surpasses knowledge' (Eph. 3:19). None of us can ever plumb the depths of God's Word (which stands to reason if God is God), and even if we were to live for hundreds of years, we would never run out of material.

So said the famous Charles Spurgeon after reading a newspaper article which expressed amazement that he could keep on year after year with 'such a narrow groove to travel in.' He responded. 'My brethren, it is not so... Had we to speak of politics or philosophy, we should have run dry long ago; but when we have to preach the Saviour's everlasting love, the theme is always fresh, always new. The incarnate God, the atoning blood, the risen Lord, the coming glory, these are subjects which defy exhaustion.'[2]

As we look at Christmas through the eyes of various characters involved, may we find an antidote to tired or jaded views of Christmas, for it is possible to approach advent with a weary 'here we go again' or even cynicism about all the 'reason for the season' messages that don't seem to penetrate the world's emphasis that it's simply the season to be jolly.

So many people see Christmas through very different eyes from those of Micah, Luke and the others.

In some cases it is seen through commercial eyes; Christmas is big business. Others see it through sentimental or nostalgic eyes. The season brings to mind family traditions, and people hark back to earlier memories which seem to take on more and more of a glow with the passage of time. Or people may yield to the feel-good emotionalism of schmaltzy Christmas movies from some never-never-land where all is sweetness and light.

Some people look through condescending or even cynical eyes. With a knowing air of superiority, they think back to plays about angels with back-to-front white shirts, rustic shepherds in their fields abiding, innkeepers who are the butt of much humour and of course the lovely little baby.

---

2   Spurgeon, *The Full Harvest* (Edinburgh: Banner of Truth, 2006 edition), 292.

They regard it all as a dream, an illusion now, perhaps with the hope that it (whatever 'it' is) must come true sometime, somehow.

Others see Christmas as a great time for the children or a mid-winter break or an excuse for parties.

May these chapters help us see Christmas through different eyes and help us all to 'keep Christmas well', as Dickens said about Scrooge at the end of his *A Christmas Carol*.

After Orville and Wilbur Wright managed to keep their aeroplane aloft for a minute at Kitty Hawk in 1903, they sent a telegram to their sister in Dayton, Ohio: 'First sustained flight today for fifty-nine seconds. Hope to be home by Christmas.' The sister excitedly took the telegram to the editor of the local newspaper, and the following day's headline was: 'Popular local bicycle merchants to be home for the holidays.' Talk about missing the point!

My hope in writing is that, instead of missing the point, we may feel: 'The more I hear the story told, the more amazed I am.'[3] This is my hope and prayer as I invite you to look at Christmas through different eyes.

---

3   From hymn, 'What kind of greatness can this be?' by Graham Kendrick (Make Way Music, 1994).

1.

'In the Little Town of Bethlehem'

Christmas through the eyes of

Micah

One of the surprising things about the Christmas story is – Bethlehem. Jesus was born not in Rome, Athens or Jerusalem, but in little Bethlehem. It would be like some big event today happening not in Edinburgh, London or Washington but in some little village that most people haven't heard of.

It happened in fulfilment of the prophecy from the eighth century BC that Bethlehem would be the place from which the King would come: 'You, O Bethlehem Ephrathah, who are too little to be among the clans of Judah, from you shall come forth for me one who is to be ruler in Israel' (Micah 5:2).

THE LITTLE TOWN

When the wise men arrived in Jerusalem, we are told that Herod called together the Jewish religious leaders and 'enquired of them where the Christ was to be born' (Matt. 2:4). They were the experts in such matters, after all, and they should know. And they *did* know. Right away they quoted Micah's prophecy. 'They told him, "In Bethlehem of Judea, for so it is written by the prophet".'

In their musical, *The Glory of Christmas*, Jimmy and Carol Owens paraphrased the story in song:

King Herod heard they were in town and had them up for tea.
He asked about this newborn King that they had come to see.
My uncle on the palace staff said they caused quite a stir
When they said they'd come to worship Him with
frankincense and myrrh.

Then it goes on:

Well, Herod called these scholars in and asked them if
they'd heard
About a King of Israel God promised in His word.
They reasoned and debated and they finally agreed
That the prophecy of Micah was the one the king should
read.[1]

Bethlehem was the birthplace of King David, and the *English Standard Version Student Study Bible* comments, 'The unlikely choice of David as king foreshadows the unlikely choice of Bethlehem as the home town of the greater David, the Messiah. Matthew 2:6 shows that Jewish scholars

---

1   *The Glory of Christmas: A Cantata by Jimmy and Carol Owens*, Lexicon Music Inc, 1980, Word Records.

of Jesus' day read this as a prediction of the Messiah's birthplace'.[2]

The familiar carol refers to Bethlehem as a 'little town', but because of the birth of Jesus it has been famous ever since, with many pilgrims making their way to the Church of the Nativity in Bethlehem's Manger Square, entering through the low doorway where you have to stoop to enter, symbolic as that is of humbling yourself before the One born there.

The gospels tell of Caesar's decree that a census should be taken, so 'Joseph went up from Galilee, from the town of Nazareth, to Judea, to the city of David, which is called Bethlehem, because he was of the house and lineage of David, to be registered with Mary, his betrothed, who was with child' (Luke 2:1-5).

It is remarkable how it all 'came together'! Registrations of this kind were not common; why did it all happen during this precise month (whatever month it was; some scholars suggest it might have been June – which would spoil many a Christmas card)? Why did it happen at the time when Mary was coming to full term in her pregnancy? It came together so that God's plan might unfurl at just the right time, right down to the fulfilment of the prophecy that the Messiah would be born in this little, not-very-significant village, and even there not in a plush boarding-house but in a stable of some kind where He would be 'laid in a manger, because there was no place for them in the inn' (Luke 2:7).

---

2   *ESV Student Study Bible* (London: Collins, 2011), 1177.

THE COMING KING

Micah's prophecy is of One who would be a 'ruler in Israel'. As we sing at Christmas, 'Glory to the newborn *King*.' The question of the wise men was: 'Where is he who has been born king of the Jews?' Strangely enough, it was also the last jibe of poor old Pontius Pilate thirty-three years later. John 19:19 says, 'Pilate also wrote an inscription and put it on the cross. It read, "Jesus of Nazareth, the King of the Jews".'

Much of Jesus' own teaching concerns the Kingdom of God, not only as a future promise but as a present reality, and one of the earliest Christian slogans was the phrase, 'Jesus is Lord'. It may sound simple but when we remember that 'Lord' was the word used to translate the holy name of God (Yahweh), and that in the Roman world it was used to refer to Caesar, we realise that it was a significant and even revolutionary thing to say. It was asserting that Jesus, not Caesar, is Lord. When *we* call Jesus 'Lord', we are acknowledging His divinity and asserting that HE – not the world, the state, material things or anything else – is our Lord.

It is His rule, His kingdom, His reign that is so desperately needed now – in this confusing and confused world. Interestingly, the journalist Melanie Phillips wrote a few Christmases ago: 'I myself am not a Christian; I am a Jew. And Jews have suffered terribly under Christianity in the past. Yet I passionately believe that if Britain and the West are to continue to be civilised places, it is imperative that the decline in Christianity be reversed.'[3]

This is a welcome recognition, although it is also true that Christianity is more than a social and moral programme. It centres in the person and work of Jesus Christ; it is that faith that is the root that produces the fruit of godliness.

The Christmas carol says of little Bethlehem: 'Yet in thy dark streets shineth the everlasting light' and that word 'everlasting' points to something else that is spelt out by Micah.

THE ETERNAL LORD

The prophecy was that from Bethlehem would come 'one who is to be ruler in Israel', and then it says, '.. whose coming forth is from of old, from ancient days.' The One who would be born at Bethlehem is the eternal Word of the Father. He did not come into existence at Bethlehem; this was the incarnation (coming in flesh) of One who has existed eternally.

When Micah spoke of 'the time when she who is in labour has given birth' (Micah 5:3), the 'she' points forward to Mary. But in a sense it was the story of Israel – a centuries-long labour before the Messiah came forth from the womb of Judaism to be the Saviour not only of Jews but of all who would receive that salvation.

When the prophecy was given the northern kingdom of Israel had been over-run by Assyria, and perhaps this comes

---

3   Article in *Daily Mail*, 23 December 2012.

from the time when Sennacherib was attacking Jerusalem - the great and powerful King Sennacherib who wrote in his annals: 'As for Hezekiah (the Jews' reigning king) who did not bow in submission to my yoke, 46 of his strong walled towns and innumerable smaller villages in their neighbourhood I besieged and conquered'. Micah's home-town of Moresheth may have been one of them. And Sennacherib wrote about King Hezekiah, 'He himself I shut up like a caged bird within Jerusalem, his royal city'. A caged bird – this is the king of Israel, God's servant, in the line of David to whom such tremendous promises had been made. It looked as if Assyria was victorious and Israel finished – but God had other plans.

And in the fullness of time, the true Messiah and King *was* born in that little town of Bethlehem. The eternal God was acting in time to open up a message that would invite people of all races to hear His voice and open the door of their lives to Him (Rev. 3:20).

After speaking of the little town, the coming King and the eternal Lord, Micah also speaks of:

THE GOOD SHEPHERD

Under God's inspiration, he goes on, 'And he shall stand and shepherd his flock in the strength of the Lord, in the majesty of the name of the Lord his God. And they shall dwell secure, for now he shall be great to the ends of the earth. And he shall be their peace' (Micah 5:4-5).

There are many biblical references to sheep and shepherding, such as the famous 23rd Psalm – 'The Lord is my

Shepherd'. Peter used this image in spelling out the message of salvation – 1 Peter 2:25: 'You were straying like sheep, but have now returned to the Shepherd and Overseer of your souls.' He was addressing the Christians of these early days and his words address us still; this is what it is to be a Christian. It is to have returned to the good Shepherd who, according to John 10, knows His sheep, cares for them and laid down His life for them. The gospel invitation is to turn from our sin and self-centredness and return to this good Shepherd.

2.
'To us a Child is Born'

Christmas through the eyes of

Isaiah

According to an old hymn, 'Many kinds of darkness in the world are found'.[1] It refers to the darkness of 'sin and want and sorrow'.

The darkness of sin is obvious enough. We live in a fallen world where sin affects so much of life, not only 'out there' but within ourselves. The Bible College which advertised itself as seven miles from any known form of sin was deluding itself. You can be miles away from casinos and brothels, but sin resides in the hearts of fallen human beings, and we know it.

There is also the darkness of want or need. This is a world where warfare and strife cause countless casualties, where earthquake and famine leave many homeless and hungry, and where physical and mental illnesses afflict so many.

And there is the darkness of sorrow, particularly sorrow caused by illness and death. It is estimated that more than

---

1   Hymn 'Jesus bids us shine' by Susan Warner, 1819-85.

151,000 people die every hour (nearly two per second). Added to this is the sorrow of relationship breakdown, cruelty and abuse, disappointed hopes, and so on.

There *is* much darkness in the world, and Christmas through the eyes of Isaiah bids us thank God for the light that shines in the darkness. He wrote, 'The people who walked in darkness have seen a great light; those who dwelt in a land of deep darkness, on them has light shone' (Isa. 9:2).

When we read Isaiah through New Testament eyes, we find that he has a great deal to say about the coming of Christ. The prophet looks forward to a day when a great light would come into the world. He puts it in the past tense – they 'have seen' a great light – as if it had already happened. It would be a time of great rejoicing, like that of harvest thanksgiving or victory in battle. In these days – as for many people still – harvests were uncertain. Many of us take it for granted that there will be good harvests, but Isaiah refers to the delight of people who hadn't been sure whether they'd have enough food to last the year but had had a bumper harvest. And when he looks back to Gideon's victory over the Midianites, he is not glorifying war but simply thinking of the joy of victory. That's how it would be when this prophesied Messiah would come.

In the previous chapter (8:20) he set out the summons, 'To the teaching and to the testimony!' For us that means: to the Bible. People had been resorting to other things – mediums and voices from the other side, and he says to them, 'Should not a people enquire of their God?' (v. 19)

There is no need for such things and the Bible warns us to keep away from everything connected with superstition and occultism. People sometimes treat such matters lightly and even jokingly, but the Bible says that these things are dangerous. It points us away from spiritualism and mediums, horoscopes and star-signs, thanking your lucky stars and touching wood. Why go in for such silly things when you can instead entrust yourself to the Lord God Almighty who has the whole world in His hands and who cares for you.

Isaiah gives four descriptions of the One whose birth is celebrated at Christmas – five in the Authorised Version (and also in Handel's *Messiah*) since 'wonderful' and 'counsellor' are taken as two separate descriptions. But most versions take it that the words are intended as four descriptions which speak of divine wisdom, divine power, divine love and divine peace.

DIVINE WISDOM

'To us a child is born ... and his name shall be called Wonderful Counsellor.' He would have looked like any other child born to a Jewish woman, yet one Christmas song says, 'The hopes and fears of all the years are met in Thee tonight.'[2] Everything about the salvation of the human race centred in Him, a baby born not in a well-equipped hospital with the best of maternity care, but with all the trauma of childbirth in such unenviable circumstances.

---

2   From 'O little town of Bethlehem' by Phillips Brooks, 1835-93.

Later Paul would write 'In the wisdom of God, the world did not know God through wisdom' (1 Cor. 1:21). We can only know Him if He makes Himself known to us. So Paul went on, 'Since the world did not know God through wisdom, it pleased God through the folly of what we preach to save those who believe.' What was preached was the message of the cross, and if the manger looked an inauspicious arrival for the King of kings, what can be said about the disgrace and torture of a Roman cross?

But, verse 25 says, the foolishness of God is wiser than men, and the weakness of God is stronger than men. The wisdom of this Wonderful Counsellor is infinitely wiser than any human wisdom and it is in Him that our true wisdom lies.

He is One who understands and knows our circumstances; He knows them better than we know them ourselves, for we are earth-bound and limited in understanding – whereas He is our heavenly Lord, infinite in understanding. We do not know everything, but He does; we cannot see the whole picture, but He can; we often do not understand all that happens, but how wonderful to be able to trust in such a Lord, such a Wonderful Counsellor.

DIVINE POWER

The second thing is: 'To us a child is born ... and he shall be called mighty God.' This is the miracle of Christmas: the mighty God came and was cradled in a manger. He laid aside the garments of royalty and came as a human being like us.

In the passage in which Paul referred to the wisdom of God, he also wrote about the power of God, the power that is revealed in the apparent weakness of the cross. 1 Corinthians 1:25 says, 'The foolishness of God is wiser than men, and the weakness of God is stronger than men.'

Paul also wrote about God choosing what is weak in the world to shame the strong, and he illustrated his theme from personal experience. In 1 Corinthians 2:3 he wrote about his own visit to Corinth, 'I was with you in weakness and in fear and with much trembling.' We usually think of Paul as dynamic and strong, but he insisted that the secret of any success was not in human abilities, but in 'demonstration of the Spirit and of power, so that your faith might not rest in the wisdom of men but in the power of God.' That is what made all the difference - the divine power of this mighty God prophesied by Isaiah.

DIVINE LOVE

Isaiah also describes the coming One as the everlasting Father. The One who is divine wisdom and divine power is also divine love. It is the message of One who would come into His own creation as one of us – incarnate, in the flesh.

It is given expression in this hymn[3]:

Love of God, revealed in frailty through the gift of a
servant King;
Sovereign power robed in humility, perfect grace crowned

---

3   'Love of God', Keith Getty and Stuart Townend (ThankYou Music, 2007).

with suffering.
O what love that calls humanity to kneel at the cross
And exchange our sin's futility for the joy of a Father's love.

This is a marvellous exchange: our sin's futility for a Father's love.

DIVINE PEACE

Isaiah calls the coming Child the Prince of Peace – *shalom* in Hebrew: not simply the absence of strife but the presence of an inner peace which makes all the difference to everything.

It is Isaiah who also wrote, 'You will keep him in perfect peace whose mind is stayed on you' (26:3) and (about the suffering servant of the Lord), 'Upon him was the chastisement that brought us peace' (53:5); and it is Isaiah who wrote, 'How beautiful upon the mountains are the feet of him who brings good news, who publishes peace' (52:7).

Paul wrote about it as a 'peace which surpasses all understanding' (Phil. 4:7), but thankfully it does not surpass experiencing. It is the gift of God to every believer – the inner blessing of the Prince of Peace.

3.

'A Redeemer Who Lives'

Christmas through the eyes of

Job

Job is not one of the characters normally associated with Christmas but he did look forward to a time when a Redeemer would 'stand upon the earth' (Job 19:25). Christmas is about the coming of One who did stand upon the earth, who was crucified and then rose up to stand upon the earth again and who will again stand upon the earth at His second coming.

The words come in one of the best-known verses in the book: 'I know that my Redeemer lives, and at the last he will stand upon the earth' (19:25).

The book wrestles with the age-old question 'Why?' Why does God allow so much suffering in the world? Furthermore, why does it often seem that righteous people suffer while wicked people prosper?

Job is introduced as a good man who 'feared God and turned away from evil.' He wasn't perfect but he sought to live in faith and obedience. Yet the first two chapters tell of the loss of his wealth, the loss of his family and the loss of his health. Job 2:7 tells us he had 'loathsome sores from the sole of his foot to the crown of his head', driven so demented that he would scrape his skin with a piece of broken pottery. Subsequent chapters tell of his sufferings, and always against the background of the question 'Why?'

It is a question echoed time and time again, from concentration camps to killing fields, in hospital wards or private homes where circumstances threaten to squeeze the life out of people and make them ask this big question.

Much of the book of Job describes the efforts of Job's comforters to explain his predicament and force him to face up to their simple message: you must have sinned grievously to deserve all this.

Job speaks of intense loneliness – 'All my intimate friends abhor me, and those whom I loved have turned against me' (19:19). Against this dark background the words of verses 25-26 stand out: 'I know that my Redeemer lives, and at the last he will stand upon the earth. And after my skin has been thus destroyed, yet in my flesh I shall see God.'

It is a remarkable text, coming from such depths of suffering, and from an Old Testament that does not spell out very much about the hope of heaven. It was thought then that people live on but only in a shadowy kind of existence, but here there shines through that hope of glory which would come to full expression with the New Testament message of hope in Jesus Christ. Through Him, human beings may live for evermore because of Christmas Day, because Jesus came to undo the effects of sin and the fall.

This glimpse of Christmas through the eyes of Job tells us of Job's faith, his hope and his assurance.

HIS FAITH

Job would have shared the sentiment of Andrae Crouch's song 'Through it all'. It talks about many tears, sorrows and questions, but the chorus says, 'Through it all, through it all, I've learned to trust in Jesus, learned to trust in God; through it all, through it all, I've learned to depend upon His Word.'

Job's faith was not in a silver lining behind every cloud; he did not simply think that things will sort themselves out some day. Rather, he trusted in a living God who is described as a Redeemer.

The Hebrew word referred to a kinsman-redeemer and is found notably in the story of the widowed Ruth. When her mother-in-law Naomi heard that Ruth had found work in the fields of a man called Boaz, she was excited because Boaz was a relative and, according to the law of levirate marriage, it was the duty of such a kinsman to take the widow as his wife, redeem the relative's property and raise up children in the deceased man's name. This was a kinsman-redeemer, a *Go'el*.

When we see Job's expression 'I know that my Redeemer lives' in that light, it becomes a precious statement - everything centres in One who came to share our humanity, to be our kinsman-Redeemer. From the depths of his suffering, Job expresses faith in such a Redeemer.

God has given no promises that there will never be storms, but Job was patient through it all because he had an anchor that was fastened to a rock, the Saviour's love. The Bible does not mock us with empty promises, but it does point us to a great Redeemer who lives and who guides His people, pilgrims through this barren land.

HIS HOPE

Obviously Job had never heard of Christmas (in a sense none of the Bible characters had heard of the concept), and the words 'He will stand upon the earth' were fulfilled in ways he could never have imagined. It's what advent is about; it is the message of the gospel, as John says at the beginning of his gospel account: 'The Word became flesh and dwelt among us' (John 1:14).

The Christian message is one of hope that is fixed on this great Redeemer. Job may have been thinking of a vindicator who would defend him against the charges of his 'comforters' who had all insisted that he must be a dreadful sinner. But the fulfilment outshone the prediction, and in the fulness of time Christ came to redeem His people from sin, evil and death.

He stood upon the earth. We can think of that in stages:

- Firstly, He came to the earth as a baby. This is the message of Christmas which is read and presented in carols and nativity plays. It is the super-fulfilment of Job's word – the Redeemer did stand upon the earth – at Bethlehem and Nazareth.

- He stood on the earth in Galilee in His life and ministry: healing the sick, telling His parables, teaching His disciples, caring for the outcasts and even untouchables, loving even His enemies.

- Then He was lifted up from the earth. The cross stood firmly on the earth and we are reminded that Christianity is not a sanitised religion that is all about white robes and stained-glass windows. It centres in the horrible events that took place on the solid ground of this earth – amid the squalor, muck and gore.

- But again, He stood upon the earth in His risen glory. He made a point Himself of saying that ghosts don't have flesh and bones as He had (Luke 24:39). Christianity stands on that belief in His bodily resurrection from the dead.

- And He will stand upon the earth again. No-one knows *when* He will come, but we know that He *will* come. He will 'stand upon the earth', and the Bible presents us with the challenge: will we be ready? That means being faithful and obedient in all that lies before us; it means honouring Him as Lord and Master in every aspect of our lives.

There's Job, this poor man sitting under the weight of his sufferings, looking for a Redeemer who would stand on the earth. *Well, Job, He did come – the baby of Bethlehem, the man of Galilee, the man on the cross, the risen One, the Lord who will return.*

HIS ASSURANCE

The first words of Job 19:25 are 'For I know'. This was Job's assurance, even in the depths of his suffering. All of his wealth had been taken from him; he had lost his family; his health was broken; his wife despairingly told him to 'Curse God and die' (Job 2:9). Yet here is this note of assurance: 'I know that my Redeemer lives.'

There may have been many things Job did not understand, but he was like the blind man of John 9 who was cured by Jesus. Jesus' disciples raised the very question which lies behind the book of Job; they asked, 'Rabbi, who sinned, this man or his parents, that he was born blind?' (John 9:2) They made the same assumption as Job's friends, and Jesus taught them that it doesn't work like that; there are no simple equations between the amount of good or evil you do and the amount of suffering you have to endure.

Job also said, 'After my skin has been thus destroyed, yet in my flesh I shall see God.' The fact that the Redeemer lives is the gospel's answer to the undeniable fact that we all die. 'Dust to dust' is the truth – but it is not the whole truth, and the Christian hope is based on the death and resurrection of the Redeemer who lives and will live for ever and who saves to the uttermost those who draw near to God through Him (Heb. 7:25).

May it be our faith too: 'I know that my Redeemer lives.'

4.

'He Will Suddenly Come'

Christmas through the eyes of

Malachi

Near the end of the last book in the Old Testament[1] we read, 'Behold, I send my messenger, and he will prepare the way before me. And the Lord whom you seek will suddenly come to his temple; and the messenger of the covenant in whom you delight, behold, he is coming, says the Lord of hosts' (Mal. 3:1).

Malachi prophesied after the return from the Babylonian exile. The promises about God redeeming His people had been fulfilled, and under Ezra and Nehemiah the returnees had rebuilt the temple and the city walls.

But life was hard, they were surrounded by enemies who sought to thwart their efforts, and many an Israelite must have wondered, 'What's the point? There doesn't seem to be much profit from trying to walk in God's ways.'

---

1   The books are in a different order in the Hebrew Bible.

It was into such a situation that Malachi came with the prophecy of a time when the Lord would suddenly come to His temple; God would act in a new and wonderful way, and Malachi spells out three things about the Messiah who would come:

a. There would be a fore-runner

Verse 1 says, 'Behold, I send my messenger, and he will prepare the way before me.' The last verses of Malachi look in the same direction: 'Behold, I will send you Elijah the prophet before the great and awesome day of the Lord comes.' This is the prophecy that was fulfilled in the ministry of John the Baptist, as Jesus said in Matthew 17:12 – 'I tell you that Elijah has already come.' John was that fore-runner, a trailblazer for the Messiah.

b. He would come suddenly

That's what Malachi says: 'The Lord whom you seek will suddenly come.' It would catch many people unawares – and not only His birth at Bethlehem. In the famous cleansing of the temple (Matt. 21:12-13) the Lord suddenly came to His temple. He took strong action to rid the temple of the clutter that prevented it being the house of prayer that it was meant to be.

c. It would not be all sweetness and light

For some it would be a day of darkness and not light, for verse 2 of chapter 3 poses the question: 'But who can endure the day of his coming, and who can stand when he appears?' In truth no-one can stand in His presence, but the point made in Malachi 3:2 is that for those who persist in wrongdoing and ungodly behaviour, His coming will be a terrible thing. The cleansing of the temple was a kind of acted parable of His coming to root out sin and evil.

These three things about the coming of the Messiah – there would be a fore-runner, it would be sudden and it would spell judgment – were fulfilled in the coming that is celebrated at Christmas. They will also be fulfilled in the second coming that we are taught to await with faith and hope.

The prophets were both fore-tellers of God's Word for their time and, under the inspiration of God's Spirit, fore-tellers of the future. And the words of Malachi spell out principles that would apply both to the coming celebrated at Christmas and to the Lord's coming again.

So far as the first coming is concerned, the fore-runner was John the Baptist. Jesus did suddenly break on to the scene and many were quite unprepared for it. And His coming was not all sweetness and light; in fact His ministry was hard-hitting and very unwelcome for many, including many of the people who should have been ready to welcome Him.

The New Testament also prophesies Jesus' coming again, and the three things that Malachi says would be true of the first coming will also be true of His return.

THE FORE-RUNNER

2 Thessalonians 2 begins, 'Now concerning the coming of our Lord Jesus Christ ... that day will not come, unless the rebellion comes first, and the man of lawlessness is revealed, the son of destruction, who opposes and exalts himself against every so-called god or object of worship, so that he takes his seat in the temple of God, proclaiming himself to be God.'

Sometimes people have identified this man of lawlessness with particular historical characters who have set themselves up against God. But, although there have been many anti-Christs (small a), *the* Anti-Christ is still to come. That coming will be a sign of Christ's imminent return. Many in the world will be hailing this apparently great leader and deliverer, but God's people will recognise him as the prophesied anti-Christ.

The Bible also says that no-one knows when Jesus will return (Mark 13:32), and we are to get on with the life of discipleship, without going to the extreme of frenzied expectation on the one hand or forgetting about it on the other hand.

A SUDDEN COMING

Malachi also said that the Lord would return suddenly. If there is one thing that the New Testament makes clear about the second coming of Jesus, it is that it will catch many people unawares. They won't be ready. The suddenness of that coming is illustrated by the picture of the thief in the night (Matt. 24:43; 1 Thess. 5:2).

C. S. Lewis wrote, 'The schoolboy does not know which part of his Virgil lesson he will be made to translate; that is why he must be ready to translate any passage. The sentry does not know at what time the enemy will attack, or an officer inspect his post; that is why he must keep awake all the time'.[2] Obviously we shouldn't press such analogies too far: for believers the day of Christ's return will be rather more wonderful than Latin lessons or being caught out at your sentry post. But the point is that we are to live in readiness.

A COMING NOT WELCOMED BY ALL

For some it will be a wonderful and glorious day; for others it will be a day of darkness and gloom. 1 Thessalonians 5:4 says, 'You are not in darkness', and Paul goes on to encourage believers to live in the light of the Lord and to be ready all the time – not by gazing into the sky and doing nothing because He might appear at any moment, but living holy lives in this world for His glory. Having received His salvation, we are to live it out (Phil. 2:12), whether it is easy or difficult, popular or unpopular, politically correct or politically incorrect.

The book of Malachi gives practical help in how to live in readiness. As we rejoice in Christ's first coming at Christmas and await His second coming in glory, there are three particular challenges from Malachi.

---

2   *The World's Last Night (and other essays)*, quoted in *A Mind Awake*, ed. C. Kilby (New York: Mariner, 2003), 101.

1. Challenge number one is found in Malachi 2:17, 'You have wearied the Lord'. It is a searching word, no doubt to be balanced by all that Scripture also says about the patience and forbearance of God. In the question-and-answer style of Malachi, we hear the people asking, 'How have we wearied him?' and the answer is: 'By saying, "Everyone who does evil is good in the sight of the Lord, and he delights in them".' It speaks of the world's upside-down morality and the way in which evil things are counted as good.

2. Challenge number two is found in Malachi 3:8 where the question is put: 'Will man rob God? Yet you are robbing me.' When they ask how, the answer is: 'In your tithes and contributions.' We are to be generous as those who expect to meet Him face to face one day.

3. Challenge number three is found in Malachi 3:13: 'Your words have been hard against me, says the Lord.' Again there's the question of *how* people had done that, and the answer is – verse 14: 'You have said, "It is vain to serve God. What is the profit of our keeping his charge?"' They had been grumbling about God not acting in the way they wanted or expected and so had come to think, 'It's all pointless; we might as well give up on faith and discipleship.'

Perhaps we have been tempted to think like that, to feel that God hasn't acted in the way we expected or wanted and so we've gone into the huff with Him – not speaking to Him, grumbling about it being futile to go His way.

There are three challenges from God's Word about how we are living as we rejoice in the first coming and look toward the second. There may be some people who need to be cooled down in their expectation of the second coming, but there are probably more who need to be reminded to be ready for it, so that, on the day when every knee shall bow before Him (Phil. 2:10), our knees shall bow not in fear and terror but in love and worship.

5.
'I am the Servant of the Lord'

Christmas through the eyes of

Mary

Most of our information about the mother of Jesus comes from Luke. Presumably he sought her out as part of the investigations he outlines in the first verses of his gospel, perhaps with the particular interest of a physician.

Luke 1:28 tells of the angel's message, 'Greetings, O favoured one, the Lord is with you.' Mary probably did not feel highly favoured to begin with – 'highly terrified' might be more like it. And as we look at Christmas through Mary's eyes, we can see various stages. First, there was her puzzlement.

A TROUBLED MIND

Luke 1:29 says, 'She was greatly troubled at the saying'. What could it all mean? Even when we allow for this being an extraordinarily special time with an outburst of supernatural phenomena that befitted the birth of God's Son, it is not every day that a young girl has an angelic visitation!

Here is the angel Gabriel 'sent from God to a city in Galilee named Nazareth, to a virgin betrothed to a man whose name was Joseph' (Luke 1:26). The virgin birth is, of course, one point at which we find much scepticism and cynicism, but really a virgin birth – or we should say a virgin conception – is absolutely the most appropriate thing, because it is a powerful sign that it is God who is acting for the world's salvation. As human beings we cannot contribute anything to that salvation. The Bible's message is a message of grace, and even so far as our response is concerned, it is God's grace that makes us aware of our sin and guilt before God and leads us to Him.

Matthew and Luke tell us that Mary was betrothed to Joseph. Today many couples live together without being married; here the opposite was true – Mary and Joseph were regarded as if they were married but they did not yet live together.

There were two stages in marriage. First came the betrothal, which was more than engagement and involved public assent before witnesses. Later there was the second step when the man would take his bride to his home. During the betrothal period, which could take place in early teen years, the couple did not live together or have marital relations, but were regarded as committed to each other – if one died during that period the other would be regarded as widowed and if either had sexual relations with someone else that would be counted as adultery.

Mary and Joseph were betrothed, so when Gabriel announced, 'You will conceive in your womb and bear a son' (v. 31), she responded, 'How will this be, since I am a virgin?' (v. 34) No wonder she was greatly troubled in her mind. The thing was impossible!

But in verse 37 we find the angel saying, 'Nothing will be impossible with God.' Of course – when it's expressed like that, that's different. *With God* nothing is impossible – it stands to reason, does it not? If God is God, there are no limits to what is possible.

The fact that Jesus was 'conceived by the Holy Ghost' tells us that He is divine and the fact that He was 'born of the virgin Mary' tells us that He is human – and it is because He is both divine and human that He can bridge the gap between heaven and earth, representing the Father to us and us to the Father.

This is what would bring peace to Mary's troubled mind. The angel's message was that she, ordinary young girl as she was, was a 'favoured one' because – verse 35: 'The Holy Spirit will come upon you, and the power of the Most High will overshadow you; therefore the child to be born will be called holy – the Son of God.'

A TRUSTING FAITH

Mary's response of faith is an example of submission to God's will. She said, 'Behold, I am the servant of the Lord; let it be to me according to your word' (Luke 1:38). She had been troubled, perhaps terrified, but she responded with trusting faith. Having become sure of God's purpose, she, so to speak, made herself available for God.

It is the attitude surely that God looks for – submission to His will. The principle may be applied to many situations and even to the acceptance of things we would rather be without – perhaps some ailment or disability, some restriction on what we can do, or a spoiled relationship we have tried to rectify but it is still spoiled, or the failure of some ambition. There comes a point when submission to God's will is the right thing, following Mary in saying, 'Let it be to me according to your word'. We can learn from Mary's faith – saying to God: Lord, I am ready to do whatever you want me to do.

It might involve something big like a change of career and taking up some kind of (as we say) full-time service for Him, or it could be in taking up some piece of service within the church. It could be putting right something that has been wrong or offering to help someone in some way that God has laid on your heart. Whatever the application, here is the lesson of Mary's response, 'Let it be to me according to your word.'

A THANKFUL HEART

Luke's gospel includes the *Magnificat*, Mary's song of praise (Luke 1:46-55). 'My soul magnifies the Lord, and my spirit rejoices in God my Saviour.'

It is noteworthy that her song is not at all self-centred. There is nothing of 'how special I must be if God should want to do this amazing thing in me'. The emphasis is on God and

His mighty deeds, not on Mary and what she would do. It is a song of praise from a thankful heart.

We all have much to be thankful for – and the Christmas message reminds us above all of this great gift that God has given us in the birth of the Saviour. How much thankfulness should there be in the hearts of those who see beyond the outward and materialistic things of a modern Christmas to its real message. How thankful the hearts of those who know with Mary what was going on at Christmas. May God give us thankful hearts.

A THOUGHTFUL ATTITUDE

Luke 2:19 says, after the events of Jesus' birth, 'Mary treasured up all these things, pondering them in her heart.' The Greek word for 'ponder' literally means throwing things together; we might paraphrase it as putting two and two together. Mary must have thought much about all that had happened: the angel's announcement, the virginal conception, the unpretentious place of confinement, the visit of the shepherds and the message, 'Unto you is born this day in the city of David a Saviour, who is Christ the Lord' (Luke 2:11). How did it all add up?

Mary's thoughtful attitude is a model for us all. Instead of rushing about like the proverbial headless chickens and going frantic with all the things that need to be done – rather, let's be thoughtful about the meaning of the Christmas event.

When we consider Christmas through the eyes of Mary, we see a troubled mind (as she wondered what kind of greeting she had heard), a trusting faith ('Let it be to me according to your word'), a thankful heart ('My soul magnifies the Lord'), and a thoughtful attitude ('as she pondered these things').

6.
'You Shall Call His Name Jesus'

Christmas through the eyes of

Joseph

Often in the run-up to Christmas there is speculation about what song is going to be the Christmas Number One. Some years ago the spot was filled by 'Saviour's Day', sung by Sir Cliff Richard. One review said, 'No snow, no Santa, no reindeer? What's this got to do with Christmas?' Presumably the reviewer had his tongue in his cheek – I hope – because the obvious rejoinder is: what do snow, Santa and reindeer have to do with Christmas?

Another song reminds us, 'Christmas isn't Christmas till it happens in your heart.'[1] Unless and until He is the centre of our Christmas, it is merely a winterval or the yuletide.

In this chapter we look at Christmas through the eyes of someone who has been called the forgotten man of Christmas, Joseph. It's in Matthew's gospel that we find out

---

1   'Christmas Isn't Christmas', Jimmy and Carol Owens (Communique Music, 1980).

most of what we know about him. We are told that Mary had been betrothed to Joseph (Matt. 1:18), and the record draws attention to three things about him. He was a good man, a believing man and a family man.

A GOOD MAN

Matthew describes him as 'a just man', using the Greek word that elsewhere refers to justification, and all that we learn about Joseph speaks of him as a man of honour.

We know that he was a carpenter and he came from Nazareth. It is usually assumed that he died young, since the gospels say nothing more about him, since Matthew 12:46 refers to Jesus' mother and brothers coming to take charge of Him, and since on the cross Jesus committed Mary to the care of John which would make sense on the assumption that Joseph was no longer alive.

But when Matthew 1:18 says, 'Before they came together she was found to be with child', this would clearly have been a bombshell for Joseph; people then may not have known about genetics but they did know where babies come from! Joseph must have been heartbroken as he planned to 'divorce her quietly'. Why? It was not anger or accusation, but because he was 'unwilling to put her to shame'. That's why he would see that the whole thing was done without the attentions of the paparazzi of Palestine! He was a good man.

A BELIEVING MAN

God granted Joseph a dream in which an angel told him, 'Do not fear to take Mary as your wife, for that which is conceived in her is from the Holy Spirit' and the record simply says, 'He did as the angel commanded him; he took his wife, but knew her not until she had given birth to a son.'

There is the faith of Joseph. He did what the angel commanded him. He took the line of the hymn that says, 'Trust and obey'. That's what it is to be a Christian. It is not a matter of believing without obeying and it is not a matter of acting obediently without trusting.

It was indeed a strange and apparently improbable message but it is one which takes us to the heart of the mystery and miracle of Christmas. The *birth* would be the same as other births but Jesus was, in the words of the Apostles' Creed, 'conceived by the Holy Ghost and born of the virgin Mary'.

Miracles were not as common as people sometimes imagine. It has been calculated that if we averaged out all the miracles in the Bible, we would find roughly one miracle every thirty years. Many people in Bible times would have lived their whole lives without ever seeing a miracle. But how appropriate that there should be this amazing miracle at the entrance of Jesus into the world.

A FAMILY MAN

Joseph was a caring husband and a protective (adopted) father. Mary would certainly know that he trusted her. Instead of accusing her of making up a ridiculous story, he loved her and committed himself to her, and clearly it is that commitment between a man and a woman that is the core of a sound and happy marriage.

As Dietrich Bonhoeffer said in a sermon at his niece's wedding, 'It is not your love that sustains your marriage, but from now on, the marriage that sustains your love'.[2] He didn't mean to take the romance away, but marriage is not fundamentally about romance. It is built on a foundation of commitment, trust and love.

And, besides being a caring husband, Joseph was an attentive and caring father. Of the little that we are told about him, we find in Luke 2:22 that, after the forty days of their purification were over, Joseph and Mary took Jesus to Jerusalem to present Him to God. And, despite the upheaval to home and business in Nazareth, he would make the journey to Egypt to look after the infant Jesus.

In a world where many fathers are absent or uninvolved, Joseph sets a good example. We should clearly do all that is possible to help and support people who are seeking to bring up children on their own, but we can also remember from Joseph's story the importance of a father who seeks to provide for his children, a father who, like the mother too, is

---

2   'A Wedding Sermon from a Prison Cell', in Bonhoeffer's *Letters and Papers From Prison* (Glasgow: Fontana edition, 1962), 150. In the same collection (p.36) he wrote, 'For a Christian there is nothing peculiarly difficult about Christmas in a prison cell. I daresay it will have more meaning and will be observed with greater sincerity here in this prison than in places where all that survives of the feast is its name.'

as concerned for the spiritual wellbeing of their children as for their physical, social and academic progress.

The two titles for Jesus in the first chapter of Matthew point to what all Christian parents will wish for their children: that they would trust and love the One who would be called *Saviour* and that they would know the reality of the presence of One who would be called *Immanuel*, God with us.

7.

'Good News of Great Joy'

Christmas through the eyes of

the Shepherds

'You don't get *Good News* any more.' So I discovered when I went to buy a box of chocolates to use as a visual aid. *Good News* was one of '10 lost chocolate classics'[1] produced by Mackintosh's from 1960 until 1988. It might seem to be true in more ways than one; the news seems to be mostly about suffering and strife.

But the shepherds certainly *did* get good news. The words are well-known: 'Fear not, for behold, I bring you good news of great joy that will be for all the people. For unto you is born this day in the city of David a Saviour, who is Christ the Lord' (Luke 2:10-11).

A well-known hymn describes them as 'humble shepherds' but the Bible's focus is not so much on their personal character as their occupation; shepherding was

---

1   www.yorkpress.co.uk/features/history/11110530.display/ Last accessed 18 February 2019

neither a highly regarded occupation nor an easy one. Shepherds had to search out green pastures and refreshing streams for their sheep in an often dry and stony land, and they had to be ready to protect their flocks from attack since sheep can't defend themselves.

THE REVELATION THEY RECEIVED

We easily miss the significance of the fact that it was to shepherds that God sent this angelic choir. The message was not sent to the movers and shakers of the first century but to 'shepherds out in the field, keeping watch over their flock by night' (Luke 2:8). It may have started as an ordinary night but it turned into a night of extraordinary events.

The hymn refers to the 'sudden dread' that seized their troubled minds and it must indeed have been an awesome and fearsome experience – but it was good news they were hearing. The age-old prophecies were being fulfilled in Bethlehem and the message came to shepherds of all people, so that they said to one another, 'Let us go over to Bethlehem and see this thing that has happened, which the Lord has made known to us.' That last phrase typifies the whole gospel message. It is about what God has made known, not something that clever people have thought up. We have it now encapsulated in the Bible, the written Word which is all about what God has made known to us.

It is also salutary to notice that this so-important announcement came to them while they were going about their regular business. They were not in some 'holy' place like a cathedral or synagogue. They were outside keeping watch over their flocks. Later, Jesus, in teaching about His coming again, would refer to servants being found at their task when the Master returns (Matt. 24:46). God does not call people to retreat to mountain tops or monasteries to await His coming, but to get on with whatever tasks we are called to do – whether it is looking after sheep or teaching children, working with our hands, serving in a shop, studying for an exam, making things – whatever it is. The way to be ready is to do whatever we are called to do with faithfulness.

THE ACTION THEY TOOK

The shepherds resolved to go to Bethlehem immediately. 'They went with haste and found Mary and Joseph, and the baby lying in a manger' (Luke 2:16). They were not going to sit for a while and consider their options or set up a committee to look into the matter. They acted immediately.

When we know what God wants us to do, we are meant to do it straight away – no messing about, no procrastination, no delay. There's a saying, 'Duties delayed are the devil's delight'. It is the devil who wants us to put off doing what we know we ought to do.

THE MESSAGE THEY SHARED

After the shepherds had visited the newborn Jesus, 'they made known the saying that had been told them concerning this child' (Luke 2:17). Making the message known is the church's continuing task. We are not called to share some theory we've thought up or worked out. It's about sharing what has been made known to us about Christ.

The good news they heard was: 'Unto you is born this day in the city of David a Saviour, who is Christ the Lord.' There are three key words that speak of what it is that we are to make known. Jesus is Saviour, Christ and Lord:

- Saviour: the Bible's story is of creation, the fall and redemption or re-creation. When Romans 3:23 says, 'All have sinned and fall short of the glory of God', it means that, as a human race and as the individuals who make it up, *we* have sinned and fall short of God's glory. Many people downplay the concept of sin or try to re-define sinful things by dressing them up so that they don't seem so wrong. But, when we look at the terrible things that happen in the world, and when we honestly look into our own hearts, we know that things are not as they should be. We need salvation – and Jesus is the Saviour we need. He saves us from the guilt of past sin, He saves us in the present through His keeping power and He will save His people eternally.

- Christ: this is the Greek equivalent of the Hebrew word Messiah and it means 'anointed one'. This Baby who was born at Bethlehem is that anointed One. Three kinds of people were anointed in Old Testament times - prophets, priests and kings – and Jesus is the Prophet who was to come, the Priest who would offer the perfect sacrifice for sin and the King whose kingdom has come and will come.

- Lord – *kurios* in Greek. It is the Greek word used to translate the holy name of Yahweh and of course it also means master. To call Jesus Lord – which was probably one of the earliest confessions of faith – means acknowledging Him as divine and as our master.

These were the names that were made known to the shepherds and which they broadcast to all who would listen. It is increasingly difficult to do the same in our world in which there are many pressures to keep 'religion' in a private and hidden part of our lives. It may become more difficult still, but Christ's commission stands. We are called to go into the world and make disciples (Matt. 28:19), to be His witnesses (Acts 1:8).

The challenge of this calling was driven home by one unbeliever in a way that makes for uncomfortable reading. Penn Teller is a magician and comedian. He is an atheist and once, after a Christian tried to witness to him, he said: 'I've always said that I don't respect people who don't proselytise. If you believe that there's a heaven and hell and people could be going to hell, or not getting eternal life or whatever, and you think that, well, it's not worth telling them this because it would make it socially awkward ... How much do you have to hate somebody to believe that everlasting life is possible and not tell them that? I mean, if I believed beyond a shadow of a doubt that a truck was coming at you, and you didn't believe it, and that truck was bearing down on you, there is a certain point where I would tackle you. And this is more important than that.'[2]

It is a challenging message from an atheist. Witnessing is difficult in our western world today, where so many dismiss the gospel as unworthy of serious consideration or simply regard all religions as niche interests. But none of our assertions of its difficulty removes the biblical challenge to let our light shine (Matt. 5:14-16). It takes patience, courtesy and consistency of life; it also needs the readiness to speak up as and when God gives us opportunities. May He help and equip us today to spread the Word as the shepherds did.

THE CHRIST THEY WORSHIPPED

The point has been made earlier that, although we are looking at Christmas through the eyes of various Bible characters, the real focus is Jesus Himself. My concern is not to point to Micah, Mary, or the Magi, but to Christ Himself. Paul wrote, 'What we proclaim is not ourselves, but Jesus Christ as Lord!' (2 Cor. 4:5) And so it is that the story of the shepherds ends with them returning, 'glorifying and praising God for all they had heard and seen' (Luke 2:20). They may have returned to their normal occupation, but in the deepest sense nothing could ever be the same again.

And it is the appropriate response as we reflect on these wonderful and life-altering events – to glorify and praise God for all that has been made known to us. That's what makes

2   https://www.thegospelcoalition.org/blogs/justin-taylor/how-much-
     do-you-have-to-hate-somebody-to-not-proselytize/ Last accessed
     30/01/2019.

'Good News of Great Joy' – the Shepherds

Christmas so much more than simply the festive season, a great time for the children or a midwinter celebration. It's a time for offering worship to Him who came not only as the Baby of Bethlehem and the wonderful teacher of Galilee but as the Saviour of all who will, in repentance and sincere faith, receive Him into their hearts.

8.

'Where is the Child Born to be King?'

Christmas through the eyes of

the Wise Men

'After Jesus was born in Bethlehem in the days of Herod the king, behold, wise men from the east came to Jerusalem, saying, "Where is he who has been born king of the Jews? For we saw his star when it rose and have come to worship him"' (Matt. 2:1-2).

A well-known song begins, 'We three kings of orient are', and it is convenient for nativity plays to have the gold, frankincense and myrrh carried by three individuals, but we really don't know how many there were and the Bible doesn't say they were kings. I believe there is a pidgin English version of the Bible that simply describes them as 'Da smart guys who know plenny bout da stars.'

The part of 'We three kings' that *is* true is that they came from the orient, perhaps Persia or Babylonia. There they had seen this special star that God had arranged. Did He guide them by means of an exploding supernova or (as others think) by a conjunction of Jupiter and Saturn?

And when did it all happen? Christmas cards and nativity plays have the wise men visiting the stable soon after Jesus' birth. Matthew says, 'After Jesus was born ... wise men came from the east' without saying *how long* after. But in verse 11 we find them entering 'the house' where Mary and Joseph were bringing up the infant. And then when Herod realised that he had been tricked, he gave orders for the massacre of all male children in Bethlehem and its surrounds who were two years old or under, 'according to the time that he had ascertained from the wise men' (Matt. 2:16). That only makes sense if Jesus could have been anything up to two years old by that time.

If we concentrate on what the Bible does say, and look at Christmas through the eyes of these wise men from the east, we see them searching and then worshipping.

SEARCHING

When they arrived in Jerusalem – the natural place to start – their question was, 'Where is he who has been born king of the Jews?' (Matt. 2:2) We don't know how long they had been on this quest or whether they might have been tempted to give it up. But they persisted, and it is interesting that their question focused on one 'who has been born king of the Jews'. This is not a common title for Jesus. It was used scornfully by the soldiers at the crucifixion who 'mocked him, saying, "Hail, King of the Jews!"' and sarcastically by

Pontius Pilate, when he asked Jesus, 'Are you the King of the Jews?' If a baby in a manger didn't look much like a king, neither did the bruised and bleeding figure before Pilate. Then, when he wrote the inscription to be fastened to the cross above Jesus' head, 'Jesus of Nazareth, the King of the Jews' (John 19:19), presumably it was his last dig at the Jewish authorities who had manoeuvred him into signing the death warrant. He was saying: this bleeding and helpless figure on the cross – that's the one you said was a rival to Caesar!

The same attitudes are still found. Some pour scorn on the message of Christmas, or at least the 'religious' aspect of it. Some are sarcastic about those of us who actually believe in the One born at Bethlehem. But, of course, there is also the serious attitude of those who want to know the truth and disentangle the facts from the materialistic paraphernalia that surrounds the festive season.

The wise men are representative of that quest of the human heart for something more than the things of this material world. God has put eternity into man's heart (Eccles. 3:11), and therefore people will never be truly contented with a materialistic or this-worldly outlook.

One of '42 wise men and women, bearing gifts of comedy, science, philosophy, arts, storytelling and knowledge' in *The Atheist's Guide to Christmas* wrote, 'Despite having lost my faith, I still celebrate Christmas and I love church music. I go to church to listen to the music. But there's a definite school of thought which says, "If you don't believe it, you can't celebrate it!" To me, it's important that people can believe whatever they like. I'm a liberal. I'm just not religious. If someone else wants to believe in God, they have every right to.'[1] At least that's a better – and more liberal – attitude than that adopted by many atheists who are very illiberal and intolerant of Christian influence and values.

But he wrote about the way in which we go through different stages:

As a child, you have someone looking after you. And then you start to break away from that, and eventually you achieve a degree of independence from your parents. Maybe humanity needed a parent and that was the part religion played. Maybe we're at a stage now where we are growing up and ready to achieve a greater degree of independence.[2]

Is he serious? Is he really suggesting that mankind has progressed or evolved to a stage where we can now stand on our own feet without any need for faith in God? Is he seriously making such a claim in this world of warfare, fighting, suffering and persecution; in this time when addiction to alcohol and drugs is such a social, familial and personal problem; in this time of violence when people don't feel safe on the streets; in this time when suicide has reached epidemic proportions; in this time of terrorism and extreme violence – and so on?

1   ed. Ariane Sherine, *The Atheist's Guide to Christmas* (London: HarperCollins, 2009), 30-31.

2   Ibid.

Is it really being suggested that we have grown up and don't need God?

The Magi from the east were wise in searching for Jesus. They were looking for the physical place where the infant Jesus was, but where is He to be found now? He is found in and through the Scriptures. As Martin Luther said, we go to the Scriptures for the same reason that the shepherds went to the manger – to view Christ.[3]

WORSHIPPING

The wise men also worshipped. They 'rejoiced exceedingly with great joy. And going into the house they saw the child with Mary his mother, and they fell down and worshipped him' (Matt. 2:10-11). He may have been a baby, to all appearances like any other Hebrew baby (no halos, etc); and these eastern visitors may have been wise and learned men, but they bowed before Him. It is a picture of the best and most fitting response to Him:

As with joyful steps they sped, Saviour, to Thy lowly bed,
There to bend the knee before Thee whom earth and
heaven adore,
So, most gracious Lord, may we evermore be led to Thee.[4]

We worship in our praise and prayer.

---

3   Unknown source; quoted in article in *Ready* (magazine of Soldiers & Airmen's Scripture Readers Association, 2011).

4   Hymn, 'As with gladness', by W. C. Dix, 1837-98.

We worship Him also with our gifts. The wise men brought gold since they came to a king, frankincense which was used in temple worship and befits a great High Priest, and myrrh which was used in the embalming of bodies, reminding us that Jesus came to die for sins (though not His own).

We worship with our praise, our gifts – and also with our lives. The outcome of the gospel is surrender of our whole lives to Him who has done, does and will do great things for us.

This is Christmas through the eyes of the wise men. In the somewhat hackneyed expression, wise men sought Him – wise men still do. If you are searching, may you find this wonderful Jesus and trust Him as your Saviour and Lord (although when you do, you will come to feel that it was He who found you). And if you have done so, may worship be your response: in praise, in giving and in living.

9.

'Search Diligently for the Child'

Christmas through the eyes of

Herod

Jesus was born 'in the days of Herod the king' (Matt. 2:1). He was known as Herod the Great but his greatness lay not in moral stature or personal popularity but in ruthlessness and violence.

When he came to power he gave orders for the execution of many members of the previous dynasty. His own two sons were put to death by royal command, giving rise to a pun; the Greek words for pig and son are similar (*hus* and *huios*) and it was said that it was safer to be Herod's pig than his son.

He was not popular, and for anyone else to be popular was offensive to him and dangerous for the person concerned. One such was his wife's brother who held high office and was popular with the people. One day when he was bathing in the royal pool with some of the king's guards there was an 'accident' and the popular brother-in-law was drowned.

Eventually Herod died in 4 BC, having issued an order (though it was never carried out) that when he died some of the most prominent people in the kingdom should be gathered together and massacred *so that* there would be tears to accompany his funeral; he realised that nobody would shed tears over *his* death.

His ruthless cruelty is best known from the so-called massacre of the innocents. 'All the male children in Bethlehem and in all that region who were two years old or under, according to the time that he had ascertained from the wise men' (Matt. 2:16) were to be killed – which was meant to include Jesus, except that He was on His way to Egypt.

When we look at Christmas through the eyes of Herod, there are three words in Matthew's account that sum up his story. He was successively troubled (2:3), tricked (2:16) and furious (2:16).

TROUBLED

Great consternation arose in Herod's mind when he heard about the arrival of some men who were asking strange questions about the birth of some 'king of the Jews'. So far as Herod was concerned, there was room for only one king of the Jews and he *was* that king. His instruction that the wise men should report back to him – so that 'I too may come and worship him' (Matt. 2:8) – could be better understood as 'so that I may come and kill him'.

Herod was an Edomite (or Idumean). Centuries earlier, Isaac and Rebekah had twin sons, Jacob and Esau. Jacob was renamed Israel, the father of those known as the children of Israel, while Esau's descendants were the Edomites. And there was the prophecy of Numbers 24:17-18: 'A star shall come out of Jacob, and a sceptre shall rise out of Israel. ... Edom shall be dispossessed.' It is one of the many Messianic prophecies from the Old Testament: a star or ruler will come from Jacob.

No wonder Herod was troubled. Any idea of a baby born in a stable rivalling his power was ludicrous, but still – something should be done to eliminate any risk.

If it seemed unlikely that that Child of Bethlehem would outlive ruthless Herod, it has appeared so to many another. There have been many other Herods who have acted as if their kingdom, empire, regime or *reich* was invincible. Dale Ralph Davis has given an illustration of the theme from the Nuremberg trials of Nazi war criminals in 1946:

After the executions of Nazi celebrities on 16 October, fourteen bodies, including those of Goering (who had 'cheated' by managing suicide), Ribbentrop, Keitel, Rosenberg, Frank, Streicher, Jodl and Seyss-Inquart, were delivered to a Munich crematorium. That same evening a container holding the amassed ashes was driven through the rain into the Bavarian countryside. After an hour's drive the vehicle stopped and the ashes were poured into a muddy ditch. Five or six years before, these men could dominate and intimidate. That night a drizzle washed them away.[1]

A TALE OF TWO BUILDINGS

In the case of Herod, there is an interesting contrast between his palace and the stable or cave where Jesus was born.

There was obviously nothing grand about the place where Jesus was born – a 'lowly cattle-shed, where a mother laid her Baby in a manger for His bed'[2].

But a few miles east of Bethlehem stood Herod's fortress-palace, a terraced building on the edge of the desert. He had built it as a hiding-place and its elevated position made it difficult to attack and easy to defend.

And it was some palace! It was larger than Egyptian or Roman palaces; it had hot and cold baths. It had a garden open to the sky and a tower from which one could see the Mediterranean to the west and the Dead Sea to the east. It had a swimming pool (where people could easily have 'accidents'!), a parade-ground and houses for servants, troops and guests.

A newspaper cutting in 2010 was headed, 'Theatre box found at Herod's palace site.' The article quoted an Israeli archaeologist's description of 'the excavated lavish private

---

1   D. R. Davis, *The Message of Daniel* (Nottingham: IVP, 2013), 107. Davis refers to Anthony Read, *The Devil's Disciples: Hitler's Inner Circle* (W. W. Norton, 2003), 922-3.

2   From hymn 'Once in royal David's city' by Cecil Frances Alexander, 1818-96.

theatre box in the 400-seat facility at King Herod's winter palace in the Judean desert. Ehud Netzer of Jerusalem's Hebrew University said the room provides evidence of Herod's famed taste for extravagance.'[3]

What a contrast between these two buildings! And who, that night, would have believed that the Baby in the manger, not the Edomite in his fortress, was the One whose kingdom would stand and grow?

There have been many Herods since, kingdoms that seemed powerful and mighty. Sometimes it seems that power – even evil power – has the upper hand, and it takes faith to believe that it's the Baby of Bethlehem who is the true ruler, the One before whom one day every knee will bow (Phil. 2:10).

And as Herod was threatened by Christmas, perhaps there are other ways in which people are still threatened by it – or by what it represents. Perhaps this is why many people are content to see it through the eyes of nostalgia or sentiment. To really come to terms with the Lord who came down to earth from heaven and who is God and Lord of all, would be demanding; it would call for changes in our lives.

TRICKED

Matthew 2:16 says that Herod 'saw that he had been tricked by the wise men'. His plan to liquidate this new King had failed, as have all plans to get rid of Him. It *is* the Baby in

---

3   Aberdeen *Press & Journal*, 2010.

the stable, not the king in his fortress, who is the force to be reckoned with.

There is a church building in Edinburgh which has a wooden cross on the wall behind the pulpit, but I noticed during advent that there was a certain part of the church from which you couldn't see the cross for the Christmas tree. Sadly, it's true for many people that they can't see the whole story because of an exclusive concentration on the outward accoutrements of Christmas.

FURIOUS

Matthew 2:16 says that Herod became furious. He issued his order for the massacre of boys up to two years old. Bethlehem was a small town; it may have had three or four hundred inhabitants, and the massacre might have been of a dozen or more children. But what a dreadful day – with 'weeping and loud lamentation; Rachel weeping for her children and refusing to be comforted, because they are no more.'

I preached from this passage forty years ago and when I looked back at my notes (I'm a hoarder) I found that I spoke then about our society being more tolerant than it was in the first century. That may have been true then, but today there is more and more *in*tolerance of Christianity and even of Christmas. The spirit of Herod is alive and well.

And we can say: if only Herod had faced up to what was happening – that God on high was acting for the salvation of people on earth – his whole life could have been changed for the better.

Christmas – the Christ of Christmas – *does* challenge everything that is wrong and unworthy in our lives, but in the deepest sense, His message is no threat. His desire is to bring people a whole salvation that deals with our past sins, our present dilemmas and our future destiny.

Herod died in his rejection of Christ (there's nothing to indicate otherwise). This second chapter of Matthew's gospel begins with, 'Jesus was born in Bethlehem of Judea in the days of Herod the king' but then in verse 19 it simply says, 'Herod died.'

We all do; we can't help it; it is the inevitable prospect for us all. And the whole point is that these events impinge on our lives here and now. Herod died – Jesus lives. All the Herods there have ever been have died, while Jesus lives.

10.
'Speaking About the Child'

Christmas through the eyes of

Anna

I was once chaplain of a hospital that had a maternity department. I was also vice-chairman of the committee of the Friends of the Hospital, and that committee had decided that a gift should be given to any baby born on Christmas Day. When it eventually happened I wanted to make sure that the chairman knew. His wife answered the phone and I heard myself asking, 'Did he notice that a baby was born on Christmas Day?'

What a question! Amidst all the activity of the Christmas season, it would be easy to overlook the main thing – a Baby *was* indeed born on Christmas Day.

One person who did notice is Anna whose story is told in Luke 2:36-38. There are only these three verses about her in the Bible but we learn several things about her, and her story is an inspiring one.

THE SADNESS SHE KNEW

Anna is introduced as a prophetess who was 'advanced in years'. She had only been married for seven years when her husband died. No information is given about the cause of his death, what age he was or whether there were any children – simply that Anna found herself a widow after only seven years, and of course in those days widowhood usually meant poverty. When we meet her in Luke 2 we find that she had lived as a widow to the age of eighty-four.

Another cause of sadness was the fact that she was part of a 'holy land' that was ruled by Rome. The ancient prophecies about God's special purposes for His chosen nation – well, there was little sign of it when Roman spears and shields could be seen everywhere. Verse 38 speaks of some people who were 'waiting for the redemption of Jerusalem'; for many that probably signified the dream of deliverance from political domination.

Anna had known much that might have deadened optimism and even squashed the faith she had. But it wasn't so.

THE FAITH SHE KEPT

People react in different ways to similar experiences. An old rhyme says

Two men look through the same prison bars;
One sees mud, the other stars.[1]

---

1   Frederick Langbridge, 1849-1923.

It's the same prison, the same bars on the window, but people look at things differently. It may be partly a matter of temperament, but whatever temperament Anna had, she had not allowed the sadness of her own loss or the tragedy of her nation to deaden her faith in Almighty God. She looked upwards.

We see her faith in two ways. First, she loved God's house. We're told that she was constantly in the temple day and night (Luke 2:37). Presumably that doesn't mean that she lived in the temple, but she spent much time there; she took every opportunity to be in the Lord's house. For her the 'redemption of Jerusalem' *wasn't* only the hope of a nationalist uprising but the coming of God's Messiah and the cleansing and renewal of the nation. Certainly, she loved to be in the house of God. It is a great thing when people love the Lord's house because they love the Lord.

Secondly, Anna was a woman of prayer. It says she worshipped with fasting and prayer day and night. She counted it a privilege to carry everything to God in prayer – whether it was the sad loss of her husband or the parlous state of the nation.

Instead of allowing the years to make her bitter, she had committed herself to prayer. She might be elderly and there might be certain things she could no longer do in God's service, but she could still pray.

So there is no tired and jaded pessimism that afflicts those who allow the passage of time to make them cynical and disillusioned. Once they were enthusiastic, full of vision and faith, and seemingly committed to God's service, but their vision has faded and they even look down on the enthusiasm of others. Robert Louis Stevenson referred to a besetting sin of old age in the 'maddening habit of wagging its head and saying superciliously, "I too in my time once came through all that", as if generous enthusiasm were a kind of childish ailment that grown-up people leave behind.'[2]

Anna was 'advanced in years' but she was still spiritually alive and vibrant. She had kept faith.

THE SAVIOUR SHE RECOGNISED

'Coming up at that very hour she began to give thanks to God and to speak of him to all who were waiting for the redemption of Jerusalem' (Luke 2:38). Joseph and Mary had brought Jesus to Jerusalem to present Him to the Lord since it was 'the time for their purification according to the Law of Moses' and Anna was there.

Somehow she instinctively knew that this Baby was special. She lived so close to God that she had an inner realisation that the coming of this Child related to the 'redemption of Jerusalem' – and, of course, more than Jerusalem, because from there would go out the good news of redemption and salvation through Jesus Christ who came to conquer sin and death and give us hope for the future.

Anna recognised the Saviour, and the same thing can happen at Christmas as people see beyond the outward

---

2   A. J. Gossip, *From the Edge of the Crowd* (Edinburgh: T & T Clark, 1924), 237.

glitter and festivities of the season, beyond even the fine music and carols - to the reality that was revealed to Anna.

The other thing about Anna is:

THE TESTIMONY SHE BORE

'Coming up at that very hour', we read, 'she began to give thanks to God and to speak of him to all who were waiting for the redemption of Jerusalem.'

Some people are given the privilege of speaking of Him, telling forth the good news of a Saviour who forgives our sins and gives new birth into His family, a Friend who promises to be with us always, a Comforter even in life's trials and troubles and a Guide for all that lies ahead. But Anna's speaking about the child wouldn't be from a platform or pulpit. She would simply take every opportunity to speak about Christ and commend faith in Him.

Today it is not easy to speak about Him; so many people simply don't want to hear. They may tolerate a bit of religion, at least at Christmas time – carols and candles are attractive – but that's as far as it goes. People who speak much about Christ may be regarded as odd or over-the-top.

Much of the time believers have to concentrate on living a Christian life and trusting that that silent witness will speak. Paul wrote to Titus about the need to live in such a way as to 'adorn the doctrine of God our Saviour' (Titus 2:7-10). Good works will never save anyone but those who have accepted Christ's salvation will show it forth in good deeds, and, whatever the world may say about do-gooders, there is no doubt that Christians are called to do good to others.

People need to see faith in action. It is also true that Christians need to be ready to seize every opportunity to speak of Christ – the Child of Bethlehem but also the Saviour of Calvary and the Lord of all who put their trust in Him. May God deliver us from shyness, embarrassment and diffidence and enable us to be always ready to give a reason for the hope and faith we have (1 Pet. 3:15).

There is Christmas through the eyes of Anna – a faithful, prayerful and thankful woman who wanted others to see in Christ the answer to their hopes and dreams.

'She began to give thanks to God and to speak of him to all who were waiting for the redemption of Jerusalem.' Whatever our circumstances in life, may we too keep faith, recognise the Saviour and speak about that Lord.

11.

'My Eyes have Seen your Salvation'

Christmas through the eyes of

Simeon

In the article quoted earlier from Melanie Phillips, she wrote about preparing for 'an enjoyable and – dare one say it – even spiritually uplifting holiday'. She referred to people who pour scorn on all the cheerfulness associated with, as she put it, Christianity's main celebration. She wrote that one would need 'a heart harder than the five-pence piece in the Christmas pud' not to feel sorry for such people - she named Richard Dawkins in particular. She is not herself a Christian but the unsubtle title of her article went for the jugular: 'Oh do put a sock in it, you atheist Scrooge!'

That phrase about an enjoyable and even 'spiritually uplifting' time certainly describes the experience that came to Simeon at the first Christmas.

Simeon's song (traditionally known by its Latin title, *Nunc Dimittis*) begins, 'Lord, now you are letting your servant depart in peace, according to your word; for my eyes have seen your salvation.' The Old Testament tells us that there is a time to be born and a time to die (Eccles. 3:2) and the acceptance of that could be said to be the struggle of human existence and the secret of peace in the face of death.

The Bible speaks of death as an enemy. It does not mock us with trite words like those of an often-quoted poem about death being nothing at all. The Bible takes death seriously as a fearsome force in human life, the enemy of God and man. Of course, it also tells of God's supremacy over the power of death and His gift of eternal life through Jesus who has 'brought life and immortality to light through the gospel' (2 Tim. 1:10).

Simeon was one of the first to see it – this (presumably) old man who greeted Mary and Joseph and the Baby in Jerusalem. Luke portrays him as someone who, through the Holy Spirit, honoured God's name, trusted God's promises and recognised God's Son.

It was all *through the Holy Spirit*; Luke 2:25 says 'the Holy Spirit was upon him', verse 26 says that it was the Holy Spirit who had assured Simeon that 'he would not see death before he had seen the Lord's Christ', and verse 27 tells us that it was the Holy Spirit who led him to the temple that day.

HONOURING GOD'S NAME

He had been waiting for so long, a kind of representative of Israel awaiting the promised Messiah, but the lamp of faith still burned brightly in him. Like Anna, he had not allowed the passage of time to take the edge off his spiritual vitality.

Some people start off well and seem very committed and enthusiastic about the things of the Lord: eager to get into God's Word, enthusiastic in attendance at every gathering where they can learn more from the Bible, keen to share in prayer, keen that others should know the good news. But later they seem to lose much that was once a vital part of them.

Simeon is introduced as someone who was 'righteous and devout, waiting for the consolation of Israel, and the Holy Spirit was upon him' (Luke 2:25). In relation to other people he was righteous and in relation to God he was devout.

Righteousness matters. No-one is saved by acting righteously; Christianity is not a Santa Claus religion where 'if you're good, you'll be rewarded'. The Bible insists there's no hope that way. If that *were* the way, we would have to be perfectly good before we could be accepted by a perfect God – and who could qualify? The Bible's message, however, is good news about God's salvation for the unworthy who simply accept that salvation from His hands.

And then, the proof of salvation is righteous living – not perfection, but the endeavour to bring every part of life under the lordship of Christ. The comedian Spike Milligan was once asked where he came from. When he replied, 'London', the next question was, 'Oh, which part?' He responded, 'All of me'! Jesus' call is to love Him and serve Him with all of our heart, soul and mind (Matt. 22:37).

TRUSTING GOD'S PROMISES

We are told that Simeon was waiting for the consolation of Israel, and verse 26 explains, 'It had been revealed to him by the Holy Spirit that he would not see death before he had seen the Lord's Christ.' Even in biblical terms, that is an unusual thing, but somehow there was such a revelation and such a conviction in Simeon that before he died he would see the Messiah.

This is what is so wonderful in this picture of Simeon taking the new-born Child in his arms and lifting up his voice to heaven: 'Lord, you are now letting your servant depart in peace, according to your word; for my eyes have seen your salvation that you have prepared in the presence of all peoples, a light for revelation to the Gentiles, and for glory to your people Israel.'

He trusted God's promise. The great thing about both Simeon and Anna is that they still expected to see God at work; they looked for signs of His action even after the many trials they had known.

The Bible encourages us also to trust God's promises – promises like:

'Though you pass through deep waters, I will be with you' (Isa. 43:2)

'My grace is sufficient for you' (2 Cor. 12:9)

'Whoever comes to me I will never cast out' (John 6:37)

'In my Father's house are many rooms; I go to prepare a place for you' (John 14:2)

If the passage of the years has seen us slip back from an earlier commitment and consecration to the Lord and His service through the corroding acids of this world's secularism, cynicism and arrogant defiance of God and morality, then Simeon's story may be a wake-up call.

RECOGNISING GOD'S SON

Here is the main thing about Simeon, this elderly man seeing at last the realisation of his hopes in this Child, a Child who was born in the normal way although conceived in a unique way, this Child who lay in the manger and who was truly the Saviour. Simeon's eyes were opened to recognise Him. He said, 'My eyes have seen your salvation'; he could die at peace.

We said earlier that such an acceptance is the struggle of human existence and the secret of peace in the face of death. How can we come to this point of accepting death – whether of loved ones or ourselves? It is through faith in this gospel of forgiveness and eternal life through Christ.

So many people celebrate Christmas without recognising God's Son; they observe the seasonal activities and perhaps sing the Christmas carols but fail to receive the true blessing of Christmas as expressed in the words of one of the best-known carols: 'Strikes for us now the hour of grace, Saviour, since Thou art born.'[1]

---

1   'Silent Night' by Joseph Mohr, 1792-1848.

Simeon honoured God's name; he trusted God's promises; he recognised God's Son. May the same be true of us.

12.

'When the Time Was Right'

Christmas through the eyes of

Paul

The apostle Paul did not write about the nativity but there are many passages in which he refers to the significance of Jesus' coming. For example, there is his exclamation at the end of 2 Corinthians 9: 'Thanks be to God for his inexpressible gift.' Paul was not often lost for words but words seemed insufficient to express the greatness of the gift of Jesus Christ, the one Mediator between God and man (1 Tim. 2:5).

There is also his reference in 2 Corinthians 8:9 to the grace of our Lord Jesus Christ who 'though he was rich, yet for your sake became poor, so that you by his poverty might become rich.'

But the title of this chapter comes from Paul's words in Galatians 4:4-5 – 'When the fullness of time had come, God sent forth his Son, born of woman, born under the law, to redeem those who were under the law, so that we might receive adoption as sons.' These words speak of Christ's incarnation and redemption and of adoption into His family, and the centre of it all is 'God sent his Son'. That's what Christmas is about – although you might not think so from many of the trimmings of a modern Christmas; the legendary visitor from Mars would probably conclude that this is simply a season for over-spending, over-eating and exulting in nature worship – trees, robins and reindeer.

It has been whimsically suggested that in the celebration which falls exactly one month after Christmas – on 25th January, Robert Burns Day – we really ought not to mention Burns too much because that isn't fair to the many other poets who have written at different times. Why should Burns be singled out? Maybe it's fair enough to enjoy the haggis and wear a bit of tartan, and maybe we could still *call* it 'Burns Day', but let's keep Burns out of Burns Day. That may parallel much that is said about Christmas.

But Paul's emphasis is that this is God's world and it is into His world that Jesus came.

And He came at just the right time. Luke 2:6 simply says, 'The time came for her to give birth', but Paul's phrase means more than that. He is referring not to the completion of Mary's period of pregnancy, but to the fact that it was God's time, planned from eternity.

There are some factors about the world then which can be seen as factors which made it an opportune time.

THE SOCIAL BACKGROUND

The world into which Jesus was born was a world dominated by Rome; Luke introduced his account of Jesus' ministry by reference to no less than five officials, either Romans or administrators within the Roman empire.

People often think of Rome in terms of ruthless power, especially because of its later persecution of Christianity, but Rome did also bring many advantages to the world of these days. There was the so-called *pax Romana*, the peace of Rome, which may have often been an iron-fisted peace, ruthlessly putting down rebellion and any suggestion of a coup, but it was a kind of peace. There was Roman law to which appeal could sometimes be made (eg Acts 22:25; Acts 25:11-12). There were also the famous roads, triumphs of Roman engineering, along which eventually the missionaries of Christ would be able to travel with the gospel. And there was the *lingua franca*, the common language. Most people understood Greek and wherever the missionaries went they could be understood as they proclaimed the message.

These things all played their part providentially in making it the right time for Jesus to be born.

THE MORAL SITUATION

Morally, things had reached a low ebb before Jesus came. Romans 1 describes the moral climate of the times. After mentioning various kinds of immoral actions, Paul writes: 'Since they did not see fit to acknowledge God, God gave them up to a debased mind to do what ought not to be done. They were filled with all manner of unrighteousness, evil, covetousness, malice. They are full of envy, murder, strife, deceit, maliciousness. They are gossips, slanderers, haters of God, insolent, haughty, boastful, inventors of evil, disobedient to parents, foolish, faithless, heartless, ruthless.' It's an ugly list and Paul went on to say, 'They not only do them but give approval to those who practise them.' (Rom. 1:28-32)

It was into such a world of debased morals that Christ came – not merely to live in idyllic Galilean sunshine, telling nice stories about flowers and birds, but to do battle with evil and the devil.

In our world, thankfully there are countless acts of love and mercy which do not hit the headlines. But it is also true that as we look at modern life there are many wrong and wicked things going on. Sometimes we might feel as if we are 'watching while sanity dies'[1], even in all the crazy efforts to denude Christmas of Christian influences, in the increasing difficulty for anyone holding to Christian principles to advance in political life, in the idea that there are certain things that are politically incorrect and woe betide those who transgress the borders.

THE SPIRITUAL CLIMATE

Rome needed some kind of religion to unite the empire and hold things together (*ligare* is Latin for join or connect). The

---

1   From hymn, 'Great is the darkness' by Gerald Coates and Noel Richards (ThankYou Music, 1992).

solution was emperor worship, which became a battering-ram that struck down many non-conforming Christians at a later time. But emperor worship was meant to foster patriotism by providing a symbol of unity.

But what good was the worship of Caesar when you had a guilty conscience or a broken heart? Wasn't there a need for something more? The Jews looked for a coming Messiah, albeit many had reformed their expectation into that of a warlike military leader who would enable them to rise up against their oppressors.

And behind all the identifiable human factors, there is the simple fact that it was the time of God's choice, the time in which He would act. In Galatians Paul refers to two aspects of what Jesus came to do: He came to redeem and He came to adopt.

He came to 'redeem those who were under the law'. To redeem means to buy back – in this case to buy back people who had sold themselves to sin and evil. The Bible's diagnosis is that mankind as a whole is fallen, that 'all have sinned and fall short of the glory of God' (Rom. 3:23). And at Christmas we sing, 'Christ the Redeemer is here'.[2]

Paul also speaks about receiving adoption into God's family. This is the amazing reality behind Christmas: through what Jesus did we can become part of the family of God. That's what the church is – the family of those adopted through Christ.

---

2   'Silent Night' by Joseph Mohr, 1792-1848.

Galatians 4:4 says, 'God sent forth his son' and verse 6 says '[He] sent the Spirit of his Son into our hearts'. John Stott has written, 'He sent His Son that we might have the status of sonship, and He sent His Spirit that we might have the experience of it'.[3] Paul says that Christian people can look to God as 'Abba' – not only King and Judge, but also as our Father.

In our world today there is much talk about 'spirituality'; it is sometimes said that many people are tired of the purely materialistic world around us and are looking for something higher, something to transcend the world of material things. If there is such a spiritual hunger and thirst, then the way is prepared for the coming of the Saviour. Sometimes it seems as if people would look everywhere else than to Christ, but if the time was right for Jesus to come and be born at Bethlehem, then perhaps the time is right today for Christ to come in another sense.

Our hope is in Jesus Christ Himself, this Baby whose birth is celebrated at Christmas but who came to do far more than brighten up the dark days of winter. He came to redeem His people and to adopt us into His family.

---

3   In *The Message of Galatians* (Leicester: IVP, 1968 edition), 107.

13.
'God Has Spoken'

Christmas through the eyes of

Hebrews

Each of the other chapters in this book considers Christmas through the eyes of a Bible character but this chapter looks through the eyes of a Bible book, the book of Hebrews. This is partly because we don't know who wrote the book. Although the Authorised Version (King James) heads it, 'The Epistle of Paul the Apostle to the Hebrews', the book has no signature and it doesn't seem like the other letters of Paul. Some people think it may have been written by Barnabas; that would fit since we know that Barnabas was recognised as an encourager of other people, and Hebrews is that kind of book – an encouragement to have faith and to beware of backsliding.

Whoever the author was, Scripture claims to be the inspired Word of God, and when we look at Christmas through the eyes of Hebrews we see several things about the Jesus who was born at Bethlehem. This chapter focuses on three verses:

- Hebrews 1:2 – 'In these last days (God) has spoken to us by his Son.'
- Hebrews 2:14 – 'Since the children share in flesh and blood, he himself likewise partook of the same things.'
- Hebrews 13:8 – 'Jesus Christ is the same yesterday and today and for ever.'

When we put these verses together, we find that Jesus is described as divine, human and eternal.

DIVINE

Hebrews begins, 'Long ago, at many times and in many ways, God spoke to our fathers by the prophets'. That refers to the things recorded in the Old Testament, and it's stated in that straightforward way: in the past God spoke. This is Christian belief about all of Scripture – as stated a few pages before Hebrews in our Bibles; 'the sacred writings are able to make you wise for salvation through faith in Christ Jesus. All Scripture is breathed out by God' (2 Tim. 3:15-16).

Hebrews goes on, 'But in these last days' – the New Testament's description of the period since Jesus was born at Bethlehem – 'he has spoken to us by his Son ... He is the radiance of the glory of God and the exact imprint of his nature, and he upholds the universe by the word of his power.' This is Christmas through the eyes of Hebrews; it's about God speaking to us in the entry into this world of His eternal Son.

C. S. Lewis encapsulated the message in a phrase from Lucy in one of the Narnia tales: 'a stable once had something in it that was bigger than our whole world.'[1]

Lewis also wrote, 'If Shakespeare and Hamlet could ever meet, it must be Shakespeare's doing. Hamlet could initiate nothing.'[2] He added a footnote which pointed out that Shakespeare could have made himself appear as author within the play. He could have written a dialogue between Hamlet and himself, in which case the 'Shakespeare' within the play would be at once Shakespeare and one of Shakespeare's characters. He suggested, 'It would bear some analogy to incarnation.' In Jesus Christ God Himself has come into His own world and He is both divine and human, both the author of the drama and a character in it.

This leads us on to the second thing we see about Christmas through the eyes of Hebrews. Not only is Jesus divine, but He is also:

HUMAN

Hebrews 2:14 says, 'Since the children share in flesh and blood, he himself likewise partook of the same things, that through death he might destroy the one who had the power of death, that is, the devil.' The first part of the verse is translated in the New International Version – 'Since the children have flesh and blood, he too shared in their humanity.'

---

1   *The Last Battle* (Harmondsworth: Puffin, 1958), 128.

2   *Surprised by Joy* (London: Fontana edition, 1959), 181.

This emphasis on the humanity of the One who was born at Bethlehem and who lived, died and rose again for us is good news. When He was born, there was no halo round His head, there were no scenes of stately majesty[3], and as for 'Little Lord Jesus, no crying He makes' – I don't think so! Who ever heard of a baby that never cried! He was a real human being. He was conceived supernaturally, but He was born naturally: a real baby who became a real toddler, a real child, a real teenager, a real man.

That's what Hebrews tells us about Christmas: the One who was divine became human. He was unique – not half man and half God but, in the incomprehensible plan of God, fully divine and fully human at the same time. He took on flesh and blood such as we have; He was subject to temptation as we are (though, unlike us, He never yielded to it); tears and smiles like us He knew.

The last verse of Hebrews 2 speaks of one of the implications of this. It says, 'Because he himself suffered when tempted, he is able to help those who are being tempted.' He knows, He understands. Another of Graham Kendrick's songs expresses the significance of it:

He walked where I walk,
He stood where I stand,
He felt what I feel,

---

3   Phrase from hymn, 'No Scenes of Stately Majesty', by Graham Kendrick (Ascent Music, 1997); quoted here in connection with Jesus' birth, although the song relates it to the circumstances around and after His death.

He understands.
He knows my frailty,
shared my humanity,
tempted in every way,
yet without sin.[4]

The one who can really sympathise is one who has been there before you, and Hebrews teaches us about a Christ who shared our humanity and who understands our life from the inside. I am thankful that from earliest days I was taught the truths expressed at the end of Hebrews 4 through the singing of the paraphrase that includes:

Though now ascended up on high,
He bends on earth a brother's eye;
Partaker of the human name,
He knows the frailty of our frame.
In every pang that rends the heart
The Man of sorrows had a part;
He sympathises with our grief
And to the sufferer sends relief.[5]

He is divine; He is human; and Hebrews also tells us He is:

ETERNAL

'Jesus Christ is the same yesterday and today and for ever' (Heb. 13:8). There are not many things in this world that stay

---

4   'God With Us', Make Way Music, 1988.

5   'Where high the heavenly temple stands', from *Scottish Paraphrases* (1929).

the same. But Hebrews tells us that Jesus Christ is constant, unchanging, faithful and dependable.

This is what gives strength for today and hope for tomorrow[6] – the promise and the presence of One who, at the beginning of Matthew's gospel, is described as Immanuel, which means 'God with us' (Matt. 1:23), and who, at the end of Matthew's gospel gave His disciples the promise, 'I am with you always, to the end of the age' (Matt. 28:20).

As we look at Christmas through the eyes of Hebrews, we see that Jesus is divine, human and eternal.

---

6   Phrase from hymn, 'Great is Thy faithfulness' by Thomas O. Chisholm, 1866-1960.

14.
'The Word Became Flesh'

Christmas through the eyes of

It is not surprising that John's gospel has nothing about Christmas trees, decorations or turkey, but it may surprise people to realise that it has nothing about the shepherds, the wise men or Herod. It does, however, contain the wonderful words of the so-called prologue about the eternal Word becoming flesh so that all who believe in Him should not perish but have everlasting life.

THE WORD WHO BECAME FLESH

Many stories begin with, 'Once upon a time' but John's story effectively begins with: Once *before* there was any time. He goes back before creation and says, 'In the beginning was the Word'. This is his description of the One who was born at Bethlehem: the Word.

A word is a means of communication. This book uses about 20,000 of them – hopefully communicating something through them. Jesus as the Word is the expression of God's being and His revelation to us.

We all reveal something of ourselves in the words we speak. If we clam up and refuse to speak, other people cannot really get to know us. This would be supremely true of God: if He refused to reveal Himself, we could know nothing about Him. But He *has* revealed Himself – in the words that He has spoken through inspired individuals like Isaiah and John, all focusing on the Word who is Christ Himself.

Verse 14 says, 'The Word became flesh and dwelt among us', and John says, 'We have seen his glory.' We too can see that glory – not in the same physical sense, but insofar as we see Jesus in the pages of Scripture and come to know Him in our hearts through faith.

It has been said that at Christmas we need the message of Easter and at Easter we need the message of Christmas. At Christmas we need the Word about the cross which reminds us of what Jesus came to do; and at Easter, we need the reminder that the One who died at Calvary was not just a martyr but the Word of the Father who became flesh for us and for our salvation.

THE LIGHT WHICH DISPELS THE DARKNESS

Isaiah prophesied a time when people walking in darkness would see a great light (Isa. 9:2). Jesus Christ *is* that light, as He Himself said, in words which must be either ridiculous delusion or the most significant words ever: 'I am the light of the world. Whoever follows me will not walk in darkness, but will have the light of life' (John 8:12).

There remain things about which we are still in the dark – for example, we don't know why God allows certain things to happen, the time of His return or what heaven will be like – but still, He said, 'Whoever follows me will not walk in darkness.' He or she will have light by which to live.

THE CHOICE WHICH CONFRONTS EVERYONE

There is a choice and it too is expressed in this record of Christmas through the eyes of John. Verses 11-12 say, 'He came to his own, and his own people did not receive him. But to all who did receive him, who believed in his name, he gave the right to become children of God.' There is a choice that must be made, a choice which is in fact made by everyone, because even ignoring the matter and refusing to make a choice *is* in fact a choice. And what greater tragedy could there be than to celebrate Christmas and reject the Christ?

One of the most popular books ever published is *Pilgrim's Progress*. it was written by John Bunyan who came from a family of tinkers, sellers of pots and pans, in Bedford in England. He was caught up in the English Civil War at a time when the authorities did not approve of nonconformists preaching. He spent a long time in prison and there wrote this book which has been translated into more languages than any book except the Bible.

A visitor to the Bunyan Museum in Bedford remarked to the receptionist on the amazing fact that a book with such a background should be known all over the world. She agreed but then admitted that, although the museum owed its existence to *Pilgrim's Progress*, she had never bothered to read it.

That is sad; how much sadder would it be to have celebrated Christmas and never have received Christ and His gift of salvation. That is the other thing we see as we look at Christmas through John's eyes:

THE GIFT WHICH GOD GIVES

John speaks about 'the right to become children of God', to be adopted or born again into His family. It is a gift for all who will receive it.

Christmas comes and goes; after all the expectation and busyness, it is soon time to put away the decorations, but it is never too late to receive the gift of God's salvation. The Christ of Christmas is the Lord of today who still holds out the Word of truth and life to us.

John also says, 'We have seen his glory' (v. 14). It didn't look much like glory amid the squalor and stench of His un-royal birth-place. As the song says[1]:

The One in whom we live and move in swaddling clothes lies bound.
The voice that cried, 'Let there be light', asleep without a sound.
The One who strode among the stars and called each one

---

1   Hymn, 'What kind of greatness can this be?' by Graham Kendrick (Make Way Music, 1994)

by name,
Lies helpless in a mother's arms and must learn to walk
again.

And the chorus of that song says:

Oh what else can I do but kneel and worship You
And come just as I am, my whole life an offering.

We are invited to come as we are. We do not have to reach a certain standard of holiness before we can come to Him or pass some entrance-exam before we can enrol in His school of discipleship. We are called to come just as we are, although He doesn't want to leave us as we are. He wants to do a work in the lives of His people making them more and more Christ-like.

Christmas is about the Word who became flesh, the light which dispels darkness, the choice which confronts everyone and the gift which God gives.

This book has looked at Christmas through the eyes of some who looked forward to it, some who saw what happened then and some who reflected on it and drew out its meaning. Jesus is THE character of Christmas. If we could speak of seeing it through *His* eyes, He said, 'I have not come to call the righteous but sinners to repentance' (Luke 5:32), 'I have come that you may have life and have it abundantly' (John 10:10). He is the Lord who says, 'Come to me, all who labour and are heavy laden, and I will give you rest' (Matt. 11:28).

COME AND BEHOLD HIM

Yes, Lord we greet You,
Born that happy morning,
Jesus, to You be glory given.
Word of the Father,
Now in flesh appearing,
O come, let us adore Him, Christ the Lord.[2]

Come and behold Him.

2   From 18th century Hymn, 'O come, all ye faithful'.

Come and Behold Him

Questions for Further Thought/Discussion

Chapter 1 – Micah

- Think of some things that 'came together' in Bethlehem to make the prophecies come true.
- What is the significance of the assertion that Jesus 'did not come into existence at Bethlehem ... (but) existed eternally'?

Chapter 2 – Isaiah

- Consider what 1 Corinthians 1:18-31 says about the wisdom and power of God as displayed in the incarnation as well as the crucifixion of Jesus.
- Could you or anyone in your group describe a particular time of experiencing the peace of God which surpasses all understanding?

Chapter 3 – Job

- What difference must it have made to Job to trust in a coming Redeemer?

- What basis is there for the conviction that after we die we will see God (Job 19:26)?

Chapter 4 – Malachi

- Many people were unprepared for the coming of the Messiah; as we celebrate *that* coming, how can we be prepared for His coming *again*?
- Consider the three challenges from Malachi that are listed at the end of the chapter.

Chapter 5 – Mary

- How must Mary have felt when she heard the angel's message in Luke 1:28-33?
- Reflect on the words of Mary's song (the Magnificat) in Luke 1:46-55. Do we have a trusting faith, a thankful heart and a thoughtful attitude as we approach Christmas?

Chapter 6 – Joseph

- Reflect on what Matthew's account says about Joseph as a godly father.
- Why is it suggested that a miracle was appropriate for Jesus' coming into the world?

Chapter 7 – Shepherds

- How can we today 'make known' the message of Christmas in our secularised culture?
- Consider the significance of the three names of Jesus – Saviour, Christ, Lord.

Questions for Further Thought/Discussion

Chapter 8 – Wise Men

- What evidence is there that God has 'put eternity' into the human heart (Eccles. 3:11)?
- What was the significance of the 3 gifts – gold, frankincense and myrrh?

Chapter 9 – Herod

- Why was Herod so worried about the news of Jesus' birth?
- Are there ways in which the real message of Christmas is a threat today?

Chapter 10 – Anna

- How can we ensure that our faith is not squashed by (a) sadness or (b) advancing age?
- Consider together Titus 2:10 and 1 Peter 3:15.

Chapter 11 – Simeon

- Has your faith grown stronger or weaker with the passage of time?
- What do we learn from Simeon's story about facing death?

Chapter 12 – Paul

- What does Paul say about Christ in Philippians 2:5-11?
- How are people adopted into God's family?

Chapter 13 – Hebrews

- Think about C. S. Lewis' analogy about Shakespeare and Hamlet in this chapter.

- What difference does it make to know that Jesus became a real human being?

Chapter 14 – John

- What is meant by the description of Jesus as the Word made flesh (John 1:14)?
- Think about the saying, 'At Christmas we need the message of Easter and at Easter we need the message of Christmas.'

Appendix

Advent Readings

The following passages of Scripture are suggested for reading during the month of December, as we look back at the world-changing event of Christmas through the eyes of those who looked forward to it, others who witnessed the events surrounding it and others again who reflected deeply on its meaning.

We begin with some of the Old Testament's prophecies of Christ's coming and then look at some New Testament passages that refer to His second coming. We consider the New Testament's teaching on the incarnation and its significance, the effects of Christ's coming, and lastly the actual story of His birth.

To the teaching and to the testimony! (Isa. 8:20).

PROPHETS FORETOLD HIM

1. Isaiah 9: 2-7
   The promise of His coming

2. Micah 5: 2-5a
   In the little town of Bethlehem

3. Job 19: 23-27
   He will stand on the earth

4. Isaiah 40: 3-11
   Preparing the way of the Lord

5. Isaiah 52: 7-10
   Good news of salvation

6. Malachi 3: 1-4
   Behold, He is coming

THIS LORD JESUS SHALL RETURN AGAIN

7. 1 Thessalonians 5: 1-11
   He will come again

8. Luke 12: 37-48
   Be prepared

9. Revelation 21
   New heaven and earth

HAIL THE INCARNATE DEITY

10. Hebrews 1: 1-4
    The radiance of the glory of God

11. Philippians 2: 5-11
    The servant King

12. Colossians 1: 13-20
    The image of the invisible God

13. 1 Corinthians 1: 21-31
    The power and wisdom of God

BLESSINGS ABOUND WHERE'ER HE REIGNS

14. 1 John 3: 5-8
    Why He came

15. Romans 5: 1-11
    While we were sinners …

16. Hebrews 4: 14-16
    He understands

17. John 10: 7-18
    Abundant life

GLORY TO THE NEWBORN KING

18. Luke 1: 26-38
    Conceived by the Holy Spirit

19. Luke 1: 46-56
    Mary's song of praise

20. Matthew 1: 18-25
    Immanuel, God with us

21. Luke 2: 1-7
    The time came for her to give birth

22. Luke 2: 8-20
    Good news of great joy

23. Matthew 2: 1-12
    Wise men worship Him

24. John 1: 1-18
    The Word became flesh

25. John 20: 30-31
    Life in His name

Other books by David J. Randall...

DAVID J. RANDALL

CHRISTIANITY

IS IT TRUE?

ANSWERING QUESTIONS
THROUGH REAL LIVES

Christianity: Is It True?

Answering Questions through Real Lives

DAVID J. RANDALL

Here are twelve real–life heroes whose stories demonstrate the truth and relevance of the Christian faith. Their stories give answers to three questions many ask about Christianity:

Is it true?
Does it work?
Is it worth it?

The lives of Columba of Iona, John Knox, John Bunyan, William Wilberforce, David Livingstone, Fanny Crosby, Mary Slessor, Corrie ten Boom, CS Lewis, Eric Liddell, Jim Elliot and Joni Eareckson Tada can inspire us because they did great things through faith.

978-1-52710-236-1

WHY I AM NOT AN ATHEIST

FACING THE INADEQUACIES OF UNBELIEF

EDITED BY DAVID J. RANDALL

Why I am not an Atheist

Facing the Inadequacies of Unbelief

ED. DAVID J. RANDALL

Eleven Christians – including a biologist, a psychiatrist, a journalist, and a debater – travelled on eleven diverse paths to faith in Jesus Christ. This book is the compilation of their answers and experiences written in response to Bertrand Russell's *Why I Am Not A Christian*.

Contributors include Donald Bruce, Alistair Donald, Henk Drost, Elaine Duncan, Alex MacDonald, Pablo Martinez, David Randall, David Robertson, Chris Sinkinson, Heather Tomlinson and Ravi Zacharias.

The authors faithfully fulfill the apostle Peter's exhortation to give the reason for the hope that they have in Christ.

James N. Anderson
Associate Professor of Theology, Reformed Theological Seminary,
Charlotte, North Carolina

For the many honest, open-minded sceptics who do want to reasonably weigh all the evidence, this book will be thought-provoking, stimulating and perhaps even life-changing.

William Philip
Minister, The Tron Church, Glasgow

978-1-78191-270-6

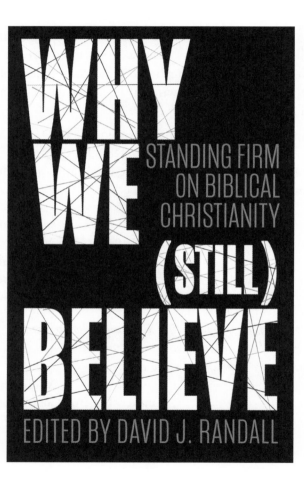

WHY WE

STANDING FIRM ON BIBLICAL CHRISTIANITY

(STILL) BELIEVE

EDITED BY DAVID J. RANDALL

Why We (still) Believe

Standing Firm on Biblical Christianity

Ed. David J. Randall

The West has become permeated with a culture that doesn't 'do' God. Many people assert that we have progressed, while Christians are still clinging to out-dated ideas. In *Why We (Still) Believe*, fourteen contributors focus on several specific contemporary attacks on Christianity, showing why they 'continue in the faith' (Col.1:23).

Contributors: Andy Bannister, Iver Martin, John Ellis, Vince Vitale, Maher Samuel, John Blanchard, Joe Barnard, David J. Randall, Stefan Gustavsson, Richard Lucas, David Robertson, Nola Leach, Gordon MacDonald, (the late) Gordon Wilson.

In a confused culture and an uncertain church, we urgently need this brave and confident clarion call. Confronting the increasingly strident challenges to faith, this is a stimulating, robust and timely response.

Jonathan Lamb
Minister-at-large for Keswick Ministries, IFES Vice President, and former Director, Langham Preaching

Instructive, illuminating, challenging, and encouraging, these pages will motivate every reader to a clearer and more confident Christian worldview and lifestyle.

Sinclair B. Ferguson
Associate Preacher, St. Peter's Free Church, Dundee

978-1-52710-088-6

Encouragement
for a young
Christian

PM. 6
POSTAGE

1ST

DATE

MESSAGES
FROM
GRANDAD

David J.
Randall

●●●○○ 📶

Hi Grandad, I got your
letter! Love Sam 😄

Messages From Grandad

Encouragement for a Young Christian

DAVID J. RANDALL

'What about making it a New Year resolution to write each other every few weeks?'

And so it begins – an amazing year's worth of correspondence between one elderly gentleman and his young grandchild. Issues and questions that every young Christian has to tackle are dealt with in a warm but direct way. This book is an essential bit of kit for the twenty-first century young apologist – or simply anyone who wants to face up to the world.

This book is full of good advice written in a very gentle way to explain to a young Christian how to defend their faith and how to live it out in a secular world. It is backed up with references to the Bible, both Old and New Testaments. In a world where Christians are often questioned about what they believe, this book would be very helpful for any Christian, young or old. The idea behind it is also a great concept for young Christians and their grandparents. I would definitely recommend it, especially as a guide to young Christians at the top end of primary school and into the early years of secondary school.

Presbyterian Herald

978-1-78191-974-3

Also available from Christian Focus Publications...

James Montgomery Boice

The King has Come

The Real Message of Christmas

The King has Come

The Real Message of Christmas

James Montgomery Boice

The birth of a king is normally marked by lavish national celebrations, a gathering of dignitaries and great joy. But what if he is born in a cave, is surrounded by animals and his first visitors are unknown shepherds?

And what if his birthday presents are obscure and seemingly useless? You may think that perhaps you have the wrong baby! The king of the universe did have an unusual arrival; the precise time, place and circumstances were pinpointed over 300 years before it happened so you can be sure that you are in the right place, after all. In this heart-warming study of the events which culminated in the birth of Jesus, Jim Boice shows us the extraordinary God who loves you and me. You will marvel again as familiar stories are explored in a way that brings fresh insight and relevance to your life today.

...challenges the unbeliever to think about the King who has indeed come in to his or her life and turned it around. The believer is led to reconsider God's amazing love in saving lost mankind, and this should lead us all to be lost in wonder, love and praise.
Evangelical Movement of Wales

978-1-84550-366-6

Foreword by
Derek W. H. Thomas

Grace Be
With You

Benedictions from
Dale Ralph Davis

Afterword by
Sinclair B. Ferguson

Grace Be With You

Benedictions from Dale Ralph Davis

DALE RALPH DAVIS

Benedictions – spoken blessings at the end of church services and gatherings – can be nuggets of gospel gold to cherish as we part from each other for another week. Here Derek W. H. Thomas has selected benedictions spoken by his colleague and friend, Dale Ralph Davis, to encourage and inspire the reader. Best known for his Old Testament expositions, Davis knows the value of remembering and clinging to God's promises.

Benedictions are gospel words. They remind us at the end of the service that we receive the blessings of God's covenant because Christ received its curses. After every service of worship, we conclude with a reminder that, as Christians, we live under the shade of the Almighty, taking refuge beneath His wings because, wonder of wonders, we are free from the condemnation of sin.

From the foreword by Derek W. H. Thomas

978-1-52710-294-1

Christian Focus Publications

Our mission statement –

STAYING FAITHFUL

In dependence upon God we seek to impact the world through literature faithful to His infallible Word, the Bible. Our aim is to ensure that the Lord Jesus Christ is presented as the only hope to obtain forgiveness of sin, live a useful life and look forward to heaven with Him.

Our Books are published in four imprints:

CHRISTIAN
FOCUS

popular works including biographies, commentaries, basic doctrine and Christian living.

CHRISTIAN
HERITAGE

books representing some of the best material from the rich heritage of the church.

MENTOR

books written at a level suitable for Bible College and seminary students, pastors, and other serious readers. The imprint includes commentaries, doctrinal studies, examination of current issues and church history.

CF4•K

children's books for quality Bible teaching and for all age groups: Sunday school curriculum, puzzle and activity books; personal and family devotional titles, biographies and inspirational stories – because you are never too young to know Jesus!

Christian Focus Publications Ltd,
Geanies House, Fearn, Ross-shire,
IV20 1TW, Scotland, United Kingdom.
www.christianfocus.com